Praise for *Drop In: Lead with Deeper Presence and Courage*

"*Drop In* is a potent and practical guide for the journey of turning inward, but there is an even more powerful aspect to this book: Sara Harvey Yao warmly and continually points the reader to foundational truths about the human experience and offers perspectives that have the potential to radically and positively shift your orientation to leadership and life."

—Cy Wakeman, *New York Times* best-selling author of
Reality-Based Leadership

"*Drop In* explains why being fully present is so hard but at the same time why it is so crucial for leadership. Author Sara Harvey Yao offers compelling perspectives, tools, and stories to help guide the reader on their personal journey. The wisdom is both tangible and lofty enough to stretch your assumptions about how to live a purposeful life."

—Christian Cocks, President, Wizards of the Coast

"Mindfulness is a vital component for a leader's effectiveness, and *Drop In* takes you on a rich and sometimes edgy journey towards deepening your mindful awareness. It's clear Yao walks her talk; her compelling personal and client stories help make this book feel not only accessible but incredibly useful."

—Tasha Eurich, *New York Times* best-selling author of
Bankable Leadership

"Don't miss out on Sara Harvey Yao's invitation to drop in! Yao is there with you page by page to challenge, inspire, and ultimately guide you on one of the most rewarding paths of life . . . a path revealed through the pages and ultimately made perfectly just for you."

—Erika Cottrell, General Manager, Sahale Snacks

"In a time of digital platforms and information worship it seems we have lost something. Sara Harvey Yao not only gives us the missing human component, she also kindly allows us access to her inner wrestling match with that missing link, Presence. The first leg of the developmental journey to awakening is that of authenticity. Presence is simply the essence of an authentically rooted and aware individual. Yao, in her work, has given us a pointer to that destination."

—Alan Shelton, author of *Awakened Leadership: Beyond Self-Mastery*

"In a society that values doing over being, sound over silence, *Drop In* is a breath of fresh air. It provides an insightful, practical framework to reconnect with our inner wisdom, based on neuroscience, Yao's work with clients, and her own personal experiences. Yao's message is compassionate, smart, and relatable. In the end, we learn that being is the most important thing we can ever do."

—Beth Buelow, PCC, author of *The Introvert Entrepreneur: Amplify Your Strengths and Create Success on Your Own Terms*

"*Drop In* is a must-read book for leaders and those who aspire to lead. The ideas on these pages are profound, transformational, and relevant, and will have you asking, 'Why didn't someone show me this before?'"

—Bret Neely, Executive Vice President, Greenpoint Technologies

Drop In

LEAD WITH DEEPER PRESENCE AND COURAGE

Sara Harvey Yao

AUTHOR OF *GET PRESENT*

[swp]

SHE WRITES PRESS

Published 2016
Printed in the United States of America
Print ISBN: 978-1-63152-161-4
E-ISBN: 978-1-63152-162-1
Library of Congress Control Number: 2016943046

For information, address:
She Writes Press
1563 Solano Ave #546
Berkeley, CA 94707

Cover and interior design © Tabitha Lahr

She Writes Press is a division of SparkPoint Studio, LLC.

To Jesse, Ethan, and Logan—
the three who offer so much meaning and joy to my life

Contents

Introduction. xi

Tenets: Foundational Principles for this Book xvii

PART 1—WHAT PREVENTS US FROM DROPPING IN 1

Chapter 1—Autopilot: The Opposite of Dropping In 3

Am I on Autopilot? Quiz. 5

How Did We Get on Autopilot?. 7

    Our Cultural Bias Isn't Doing Us Any Favors 7

    Our Brain Is Conditioned to Be on Autopilot. 13

    We Are Wired to Avoid Emotional Discomfort. 18

Summing Up Autopilot. 21

Chapter 2—Being Present: A New Foundation of Awareness . . 23

What Is Presence?. 27

Present-Moment Awareness. 29

    Experimenting with Present-Moment Awareness 32

Chapter 3—The Presence Tug-of-War 47

Safety in the Status Quo 48

Moving Beyond the Status Quo 50

The Reactive State 52

    The Three Reactive Tendencies 56

The Mind's Spell 64

A New Perspective 67

Part 1 Reflection 72

Interlude—The Revealing of Stable Ground 75

PART 2—ACCESSING CLARITY, CONNECTION,
     AND COURAGE 81

Chapter 4—Accessing the Clear Mind 85

Gathering Attention 87

    The Why of Stillness 88

    Setting the Stage for Meditation 93

Progressive Meditation Experiments 100

Acknowledging Mind Stories 106

Tools for Working with Mind Stories 109

Chapter 5—Accessing Your Connected Heart 115

The Transformational Power of Listening 116

The Underpinnings of True Listening 117

The Art of Nondoing 119

The Art of Nonknowing 120

The Art of Nonattachment 121

Deep Listening 124

Listening to Yourself 125

Experiments in Deep Listening to Self 128

Listen for Silence 128

Listen for Insight 128

Deeply Listening to Others 129

Experiments When Listening to Others 131

Uninterrupted Listening 131

Share What Is There 132

Turning Toward Emotion 133

Emotional Maturity 134

Dropping into Emotion 136

The Journey of Dropping into Emotion 137

Step In 138

Rest into the Emotion 138

What's Even Deeper? 139

Give Voice to the Emotion 139

Let It Flow 139

Acknowledge Yourself 140

Tools for Connecting to Heart 141

Gratitude 141

Assuming Decent Intent 141

Goodwill Meditation 142

Chapter 6—Accessing Your Courageous Gut 145

Incremental Courage 146

Claiming Space 148

Choosing Space 149

The Value of Prioritizing 152

Tools for Claiming Space 154

Calendar Reflection 154

Saying No 156

White Space 157

Family White Space 158

Aligning Action with Awareness 158

Surrendering to Awareness 159

Tools for Aligning with Awareness 163

Put Yourself in the Field of Presence 163

Take the Very Next Step 164

Get Support 165

Body Integration 165

Part Two Reflection 166

Chapter 7—Going Forward in the World 169

Tell Me What to Do 170

The Hero's Journey 171

Own Your Journey 175

Notes 177

Acknowledgments 181

About the Author 183

Introduction

WHEN I STARTED WRITING my first book, *Get Present: Simple Strategies to Get Out of Your Head and Lead More Powerfully*, I had visions of it being a robust and comprehensive volume about the power of present-moment awareness as it particularly related to leadership. *Get Present* had a life of its own and, as it turned out, came forth as a quickly digestible, fit-in-your-purse-size book that did a great job of introducing the concept of presence to leaders. It was a tasty appetizer, not a full entrée.

As I took the book out to corporations, schools, and other social organizations, the concept of being present resonated with every audience I spoke with. I received hundreds of e-mails and comments from people telling me they were practicing being present at work, at home, and with themselves. People would stop me in hallways where I was consulting and say things like, "Hey, Sara, I'm present right now. Isn't it awesome?" or, "I was totally present in my last meeting, and I think my boss noticed." At first I was pleased to hear that being (more) present was helping people, but the more comments I received, the more I felt something was off. I couldn't figure out why these seemingly positive and benign comments were bothering me.

When I got curious about my agitation, I realized it wasn't the comments themselves that were the issue; it was the energy behind them. The people who stopped me in the hallways were telling me about how present they had been in meetings, but it was obvious when they talked to me that they were still quite amped and adrenalized. They spoke quickly, had a hard time maintaining eye contact, and were in a hurry to get to their next meeting. After watching this pattern for a while, I figured out that part of my frustration was that people were taking the "concept" of presence and reducing it to yet another "tool" to get ahead, accomplish more, or just generally feel better about themselves.

I didn't back off from my frustration, because I've learned through my own work that when I get agitated or frustrated, it's often the fuel I need to drive my investigation into the real gem under my initial reaction. When I talked to my coach about my experience of being frustrated, she eventually asked me, "What do you really want to express?"

I blurted out quite emphatically, "Presence isn't a thing you do. It's the essence of who you are! We're so conditioned to think we have to do something, but the whole gig here is that we just *are* pure presence and awareness." I was surprised by my clarity and forthrightness in that moment, but I knew I had hit on a truth that I couldn't ignore. I did some more processing with my coach, and after the surge of energy started to subside, I confessed, "I just want to help people cut through their fog so they can remember who they really are."

What I knew then, and know even more so now, is that *Get Present* was only the tip of the iceberg of what I hoped to express about the journey of remembering our true nature of presence. Presence is and will forever be the foundation you need to feel your natural state of clarity, calm, courage, and compassion. It's just that we have a lot of stuff standing between our monkey-mind conditioned state and our natural state of presence.

We come into the world fully present in a new human body and then get plopped into a family with varying levels of dysfunction (and, yes, *all* families are dysfunctional at some level). Then we quickly adopt reactive behaviors in order to survive and thrive in the unique dynamics of our environment. All those learned behaviors (our conditioning) create a fog, and the more time passes and the more experiences we have, the fog gets so thick that we forget our natural state of presence. It's the human condition to forget that we are presence in human form. We forget that behind the chatter of our mind and the constant movement of our bodies is a fundamental silence and awareness that is always available. So the game is to forget and remember as often as we need to until we realize that we are inherently presence and there isn't another thing we have to do to get "there" in life, other than remember the essence of who we are.

When I first heard teachers speaking about presence (also often referred to as our natural state or pure awareness), I had no idea what they were talking about. Because I didn't understand right away, my mind became bored and judged my teachers as "woo-woo" and not grounded in my reality. Yet, even though my mind made judgments, there was something deeper in me that felt compelled to keep coming back and learning—even if part of me didn't get it. My curiosity and intuition kept me moving forward through some pretty sticky internal stuff, and I learned a few things along the way about what it means to "drop in" and what's required to cut through the fog of our conditioning.

Dropping in starts with present-moment awareness. With present-moment awareness, you can spot the mental patterns that fog your clarity. You can identify your thoughts and navigate through them to access a newfound clarity. The further you drop in, the more you can access, identify, and work with your emotional patterns. You can efficiently metabolize emotions and access a profound level of compassion for yourself and others. Even deeper in, you can access your gut sense and draw from the wisdom and courage of your deeper essence. Dropping in means that your full system is online, guiding you with an unprecedented level of awareness, precision, and internal stability.

Initially, dropping in may feel like something you need to learn how to do or practice to get right. The counterlogical aspect of dropping in is that you don't need to learn how to do it. Dropping in is a state of being, not another thing you do. You simply need to allow for a certain level of undoing to let awareness and presence reveal themselves to you. If there is anything to "do" here, it's having a clear intention and the courage to take action to create the space you need to feel your abiding presence.

Have you ever experienced a situation where you were losing sleep worrying about something you couldn't control? Or you just couldn't shake an emotion and it clouded your whole day? When you are dropped in, your thoughts, emotions, and external situations no longer take you on an involuntary roller coaster ride. Don't get me wrong—being dropped in doesn't mean you are void of feeling or thought. Quite the contrary. When you drop in, you are acutely aware of your thoughts, emotions, and environment, but you also have access to a deep inner stability that helps you stay steady and grounded in the midst of the reaction. You have a sense of being fundamentally okay. You are resilient, clear, and able to spontaneously respond to anything being thrown at you. Your "happiness" is no longer dependent on your external situation; instead, you access your preexisting deep sense of well-being.

Dropping in fundamentally requires a shift in your orientation to the world. Many of us are deeply rooted in our orientation to the external world to provide us with a sense of happiness, worth, stability, and safety. We look to promotions, awards, material items, relationship status, number of friends on Facebook, and so on to (at some level) give us a sense of identity and worth in the world. When you drop in, the external world becomes less relevant as you shift your orientation inward. Instead of allowing the uncontrollable external world to dictate your level of happiness or stress, you now have an internal reference point that provides the only real source of stability and peace: presence.

This book is intended to support those of you who are curious and courageous enough to start exploring your inner world more deeply. It's not a how-to book as much as it is a guidebook with some pointers to help you navigate your journey with a bit more ease. In fact, given how our culture loves prescriptions, I think it's important that we cover what you should and should not expect:

This book *will not*:
- Provide an x-step solution for all your problems
- Change you overnight
- Promise to make you richer, better-looking, or more important in the world
- Sugarcoat the truth of what you need to fully drop in or what might happen when you do

This book *will*:
- Give you perspective to help you drop into your natural state of presence and awareness
- Point you back to a preexisting state of clarity and well-being
- Offer tools to help ground your new perspective and orientation as you engage in your daily life
- Act as a reference point of clarity and support that you can keep coming back to as you go forward in life

I write about this journey both from my vantage point of walking others through their own journeys and because I'm (still!) on the journey myself. Throughout my early years, I learned that if I worked hard, I could create a sense of control. I became extremely focused on attempting to control, and, as a result, I attempted to control every aspect of my life from pretty early on. Then, when I entered the work world and found out I could get rewarded for my obsession with control, I was off and running and created a "successful" life, complete with a master's degree, a good paycheck, awards at work, a fulfilling marriage, a beautiful home, and lots of friends.

Little did I know that, after I quit my last corporate job, as an internal leadership director; had my first son, in 2002; and started my consulting business, my gig of controlling things and "making stuff happen" would start to unravel quickly. My last fourteen years, of business ownership, parenting, and working with thousands of leaders across the globe, have provided me with a profound opportunity to deepen my understanding of presence and our natural state. I don't—and can't—write this book from "on top of the mountain"; rather, I write as a fellow seeker who, like everyone else, has to remember to come out of the fog. I hope I can be of help as you, too, start to see your life more clearly.

Tenets:

Foundational Principles for This Book

WHEN YOU DROP INTO a deeper level of presence and awareness, you will likely feel you are in new territory. Your new perspective and clarity may feel unfamiliar and counter to what you have always done or have been trained to do. There may be a part of you that intuitively gets the concept of being present but at the same time resists exploring presence at a deeper level than the conceptual mind allows. *Drop In* dives into this internal tug-of-war and shows you how to work with it. But before we drop in too deeply, I want to offer a few foundational tenets, or principles, you can use to help navigate the new internal terrain you may find yourself in as you work through this book (and life). If at any time you feel disoriented, confused, irritated, overwhelmed, or even scared, just come back to these tenets and see if you can sense the clarity and stability they offer.

Your mind may think some (or all) of these tenets are too good to be true, or that they just don't make sense, and that's fine. Notice your mind's commentary, but don't give it your full attention. Instead, shift your attention to a part of you that may not get a lot of airtime: your inner wisdom. As you read these tenets, allow yourself to imagine them as true possibilities and see what it feels like. You may be surprised to discover that a part of you intuitively understands the potency of these tenets, even when your mind doesn't understand how they could possibly be true. Note that these tenets are not designed to speak to your analytical or conditioned mind. Instead, they speak to your heart, your soul, your gut, and the part of you that is far wiser than your intellectual mind.

Think about these tenets as things you can come back to in order to reorient yourself as you go through the process of dropping in that's core to this book. Even more important, these are principles you can use to relate to your entire life, however it unfolds for you. With that said, rest and breathe into these tenets and let them soak into your awareness.

- **Preexisting condition of presence.** You came into this world as an aware, present, and curious being, and this is your natural state. Beyond the constant commentary of your mind, and beyond the ups and downs of your emotional state, you *are* pure presence and awareness. Even though you may not access your natural state very often, that doesn't mean it doesn't exist.

- **Life is always happening.** There is a constant flow in your life, regardless of what you do or don't do. Like a river current, creative life-force energy is moving through you, regardless of your "effort." You are not responsible for keeping the water flowing, nor can you dictate where the river goes. It's going to go where it wants to go, with or without your permission or approval, and the same is true of life-force energy. It's about aligning yourself with the flow of the current, instead of resisting it.

- **Lacking nothing.** You don't need to compensate for what you are lacking, or get any more external validation or knowledge, to return to your natural state of presence. When you return to your natural state of pure awareness and presence, you will remember that you are already whole and don't need "fixing" in any way. This doesn't mean you won't continue to learn and grow, but your desire to learn won't originate from a sense of lack.

- **You are not your thoughts or emotions.** We are conditioned to place our attention on the *content* of minds (our emotions, thoughts, external experiences) and then mistakenly build our identity around that content. When you expand your attention beyond the content of your mind, you will access a preexisting condition of presence and awareness. Awareness is the *context* in which your experience happens— meaning, all the content you experience happens within a broader context of awareness, presence, or silence. Just beyond our thoughts and emotions lies a stillness, quietness, or silence that is always available to you, regardless of your external situation.

- **Being at choice about where you put your attention.** If you wonder what is important to you, simply look at where you put your attention and awareness. If you notice that you give your attention to things in your life that are not nourishing to you, you can change it. You can make a choice to turn your attention inward. You can make a choice to put down your phone and be still and silent for a few minutes. Your experience of life comes down to moment-by-moment choices, and the beautiful thing is that you are in control of many of those choices. No matter how busy you are, you are fully capable of creating the space you desire to drop into the clarity of your mind, connectedness of your heart, and courage of your gut.

- **Nothing replaces stillness and silence.** Our busy lives fragment our attention and energy, often to the point where we cannot relax or focus on any one thing at a time. Being in silence and stillness, even if only for a few minutes, is a way of gathering your attention and energy. You can't access insight or clarity when you are constantly running from one thing to the next. When you are silent and still, you have a far better chance of noticing the depth and clarity of your preexisting state of presence.

- **Action will emerge from inspiration.** As you rest into your natural state of presence and awareness, you will access greater clarity and vitality. From the state of presence, you will be moved to take spontaneous and inspired action. Flowers don't will themselves to bloom, nor do babies will themselves to crawl; it just happens as a natural and organic process. As you deepen your awareness, your need for "self-will" to drive action will naturally give way to inspiration and intuitive knowing.

Now, close your eyes and tune into your internal experience of reading these tenets. First, what do you notice in your body? What thoughts or emotions come up for you? Take as much time as you want to let your mind, heart, and body sift through these tenets.

The point of this book is to guide you in your own inner exploration. The way you responded to these foundational principles will inform your journey. Where you are right now is not unlike being at a trailhead of a cool and rigorous hike. If you notice the weather is stormy or the trail has a tree across it, don't take it personally; it's just information that you will work with. Your initial responses (and all of your responses throughout the book) are just data about how your system is absorbing the material and are not to be taken too seriously. If you noticed resistance, be gentle and don't try to force yourself through this book; take it bite by bite, and let your system digest it at its own pace. If you noticed that reading these tenets inspired you, then use this information to propel you through the rest of the book, especially when your resistance pops up.

I will reference these tenets throughout the book and give you tools and experiments to engage with, but the good news is that the journey of inner exploration has no end, so you don't have to be in a hurry to get to the finish line. Remember that ultimately this inward journey is yours and these tenets are something you must investigate on your own to see whether or how they are true for you.

Take your time and enjoy the journey.

PART 1—WHAT PREVENTS US FROM DROPPING IN

We should take care not to make the intellect our god; it has, of course, powerful muscles, but no personality. It cannot lead; it can only serve. —Albert Einstein

IN ORDER TO EXPERIENCE clarity and presence, we first need to know what is getting in the way of them—and there is a lot that gets in the way! If this were an easy process, everyone would be doing it. In fact, the process to acknowledging clarity and awareness isn't particularly easy, and your rational mind alone probably won't be able to sustain the journey.

In my own experience, and based on what I see in others, the hunger for presence doesn't come from the conditioned or rational mind alone. In fact, our conditioned minds are just that—conditioned and operating on autopilot. It's nearly impossible for the conditioned mind to want something else, when its orientation is to the status quo.

The desire for clarity and connection originates from something far deeper than your mind. People refer to this energy as their soul, creative energy, God, or simply pure presence. In the spring of 2015, my youngest son asked me how flowers and trees "know" when to bud and bloom. He was perplexed, he said, because flowers and tress "don't have brains." Of course, that opened up a rich conversation about wisdom beyond the brain, but his question points to a very important aspect of our existence. Many of us have times in our lives when we feel drawn to explore our inner worlds. Sometimes this process is initiated by an external situation, like the loss of a job or a loved one, or by some other crisis. Other times, the urge is spontaneous and often doesn't make sense to our rational mind—and it doesn't need to.

In this first part of the book, we will dive into our collective social and cultural conditioning, as well as the physiological aspects of our human makeup that get in the way of our dropping in. When we are not operating from presence, we are essentially unconscious. The only way you can move through unconsciousness is to learn what got you there in the first place (your conditioning) and then how to make a more informed decision about moving beyond your conditioning. As you read this part of the book, consider that the struggle of staying present and aware is part of the human condition. May you find compassion for yourself and others as you see the bigger picture of how and why it's so common to operate on autopilot and what it takes to move beyond it.

CHAPTER 1—Autopilot: The Opposite of Dropping In

The truth will set you free, but first it will piss you off.
—Gloria Steinem

ONE OF MY MORE POWERFUL wake-up calls came in October 2009. For several weeks prior, I had been under incredible stress at work. I had been leading a new and very visible leadership team development project in which I had several tight deadlines and lofty deliverables. I also had several high-visibility keynote-speaking events booked. My son was starting at a new school, and I had a low-grade respiratory cold I couldn't quite shake. I remember having moments of thinking I should slow down and rest, but I quickly brushed that inner voice to the side in the name of productivity.

On car rides home from work during that time, my mind was constantly spinning. I was dissecting what I had said in my last big meeting. I was worried about what I was going to say in my next keynote. I painfully deliberated over what I was going to wear at every event, and I wondered how my son was doing at school.

Morning, noon, and night, my mind was strategizing, analyzing, and mostly worrying. I was exhausted.

On October 29, 2009, I spoke to a room of 1,100 people at Microsoft right before its then-CEO, Steve Ballmer, took the stage. I delivered a great keynote titled "Succeeding Without Side Effects" and promptly came home and physically crashed. I woke up the next day and took a gulp of water, but instead of swallowing it, I felt the water dribbling down my face. When I wiped away the water, I couldn't feel my fingers on my face. Then sheer panic overtook me as I realized I couldn't feel *anything* on the entire right side of my face. The sensation was similar to a novocaine shot.

I immediately called my doctor and made an emergency appointment. She informed me matter-of-factly that I had Bell's palsy, a virus that's related to the Epstein-Barr virus (mono) and that paralyzes one side of the face. She told me how in good cases the paralysis is temporary, lasting three to four months, and in not-so-good cases is permanent.

Needless to say, I was terrified. I later learned that Bell's palsy is most commonly brought on by stress. My doctor explained that it's an opportunistic virus that takes over when your immune system is compromised over a period of several weeks. I walked out of her office stunned and scared. When I arrived home and really took a good look at my face, my heart sank. The entire right side of my face hung a bit lower than the left. When I tried to smile, the left side of my face lifted up, but the right side was frozen.

I was unable to close my eyelid and had to put eye drops in every hour and wear an eye patch so I wouldn't lose my eyesight. I couldn't eat or drink without food and water falling out of my mouth; I couldn't talk without sounding a little tipsy. I was still exhausted and slept for four to six hours during each day, on top of the eight to nine hours of sleep I got each night, hoping I would have enough energy to be with my kids when they got home from school. I had been living my life on autopilot and was feeling the effects of it—big-time. Needless to say, I was not succeeding without side effects.

Living on autopilot is essentially the opposite of being dropped in. When you're on autopilot, you're living in an unconscious state. You're going through the motions of life, checking things off your list, but not being really, truly present to your experience. When you're living on autopilot, there's not a lot of room for questioning much of anything. Your conditioned mind convinces you that you must keep going, pushing, striving, producing, grasping, and proving your value. In quiet moments, the small voice of deep wisdom inside you may start questioning what you're doing, just as mine started to question me, but living on autopilot tends to squash down or altogether ignore that wisdom in the name of keeping the status quo. After all, who would we be if we weren't powering through?

Am I on Autopilot?

The great news is that if you're asking yourself the question "Am I on autopilot?" you are (at least momentarily) not on autopilot. However, it's common to come in and out of awareness by having moments of presence and then a whole lot more moments on autopilot. The tricky thing about being on autopilot is the unconscious nature of it. Think about how autopilot works in a jet: the pilot decides to put the plane on autopilot and then in theory can rest, sleep, or take a break while someone or something else monitors the controls. That's kind of what we do. We essentially put our lives on autopilot and then go to sleep at the wheel. Our lives keep going in some direction, but we're not really stewarding the direction with much conscious awareness.

On a jet, the pilot has to make a decision to take the aircraft off autopilot and take back the controls. But how do we do that for ourselves if we don't even know we're on autopilot? It's a conundrum both to be the one asleep *and* to have to be the one to wake up. This is where your motivation for waking up becomes very important. If your motivation for staying on autopilot is stronger than your desire to wake up, you may be set up for a long haul of unconsciousness.

The following are some signs we can look at to tell us if we're living on autopilot. Perhaps you can relate?

- You have a hard time going to sleep or staying asleep because your mind is thinking about the past or the future.
- You get lost in worry, overthinking, and analyzing far more than you'd like and have a hard time turning it off.
- You don't notice (or do notice but power through) body aches, pains, or illnesses.
- You don't hear what your coworkers, children, or partner is saying because you are distracted.
- You miss out on time with loved ones because you're so busy.
- You're irritated, cranky, or in a bad mood and don't really know why.
- You don't get the amount of sleep or exercise you'd like because of how busy you are.
- On some level, you feel as if your life is in control of you, versus your being in control of your life.
- You have no regular space in your calendar to reflect or simply "be."
- You get sick more than you'd like.
- Your love relationship is strained, but it's easier to ignore or avoid the real issues.
- You're behind on routine self-care, such as doctor and dentist appointments.

- You have a faint but nagging feeling that something about your life is "not right."
- When you think about making a change, it feels overwhelming, so you keep on doing what you're doing.

If you answered yes to several (or most) of these statements, you're not alone. Unfortunately, operating on autopilot has become more of the norm, yet it is having devastating effects on our health, happiness, and effectiveness. The beautiful thing is that we don't have to live like robots on autopilot. The rest of this book is dedicated to how we can wake up and stay awake and navigate our lives from a place of presence and well-being.

How Did We Get on Autopilot?

Operating on autopilot seems to be, at least on some level, a universal human experience. Not only are our primitive brains wired to be on autopilot, but our culture, in recent history, has reinforced the concept. As we look at our historical, physical, cultural, and psychological biases toward autopilot, it's understandable that we are a society that is swimming upstream when it comes to living from presence. However, this is changing. Even in the last five years, conversations about consciousness, mindfulness, presence, and awareness are increasing in just about every field and industry.

Our Cultural Bias Isn't Doing Us Any Favors

Our cultural bias toward valuing the rational mind over inner awareness can be traced back to the age of reason, which took hold during the seventeenth century. Renowned philosopher René Descartes laid the foundation for the theory of rationalism, reflected in the famous statement "I think, therefore I am." Rationalism states that the truth is based not on sensory experience but on intellectual understanding.

Rationalism was an important developmental stage for the Western world. Many of our historical advancements happened as a result of our proving theories based on objective evidence, such as the fact that the world is round, instead of flat, and that the earth revolves around the sun, not the other way around. Without objective and rational evidence, many of our scientific and societal advancements might not exist.

The foundation of rationalism remains deeply entrenched in our society today, as the US educational system, for example, clearly evidences. Although this system is arguably still falling short in the area of properly developing our children's intellectual capacity, what is even more obvious is how little (if any) focus there is on developing other forms of intelligence and awareness. Elementary schools throughout the country are cutting programs like music, physical education, and even recess in favor of spending more time developing the intellect. Music and PE classes and recess are some of the only times when children have an opportunity to experience sensations in their bodies and the outdoors and to develop other important forms of intelligence, like emotional, social, and body awareness. Cutting these programs points to our deep bias toward the rational mind and to our underlying assumption that the intellect trumps other forms of intelligence.

Science is another realm in which rationalism rules our culture. Materialist science, meaning primarily a focus on physical or atomic matter, has dominated what scientific research deems "acceptable" or "objective" and consequently has shaped our collective view and socially accepted paradigms of scientific reality. However, since we now understand that the universe is made up of only about .01 percent atomic matter, it is the other 99.9 percent of the invisible universe that is starting to get more attention. In fact, many believe that science itself is in the early stages of a significant revolutionary shift. We are moving into a new scientific world that includes energy, the quantum realm, consciousness, qualia or phenomenology, and rigorous first-person contemplative inquiry. This will have a revolutionary impact on the areas of medicine, physics, psychology, physiology, cosmology, and more.

There is no denying that the rational or analytical mind is a very powerful tool and should be utilized, but it's important to remember that it's just that—a tool—not our entire reality. As with any powerful tool, the rational mind can produce great results when directed and leveraged with intention and clarity, but it can be equally unproductive and damaging to results when not guided by wisdom.

There are several ways in which American culture both reinforces and rewards the misuse of the rational mind and ultimately erodes productivity, bottom-line results, innovation, and our fundamental sense of well-being.

Multitasking

One example of a way in which our culture reinforces the misconception of productivity is its emphasis on the effectiveness of multitasking. We are taught to "get more done, faster," and many of us believe multitasking helps produce better results. Yet multiple studies indicate that multitasking has the opposite effect. We lose up to 40 percent of our effectiveness when we multitask—meaning we miss details, make mistakes, and produce less work. In fact, the same studies show that the better people think they are at multitasking, the less effective they are.[1]

I often see people multitasking during meetings, and it commonly erodes results, as opposed to improving them. Most of the companies I work with accept and sometimes even encourage the use of a laptop, tablet, or phone during meetings, in order for their employees to be more "productive." However, it's common for the meeting leader to jump right in without making eye contact with the participants, and to even skip over the purpose and objectives of the meeting. When the meeting leader attempts to initiate a constructive conversation, a few key players join in, while others are heads down in their e-mail. It's not unusual for me to see someone who has been working on their laptop for a good portion of the meeting lift their head twenty to thirty minutes into it to try to figure out what the group is talking about. Then, when they get the gist of it, they speak up with a new data point or question that would have been far more appropriate and productive to hear earlier in the conversation, or, much to their embarrassment, they realize someone else has already made that same point. These individuals are under the illusion that doing their e-mail during a meeting is productive, but what really happens is that the meeting goes long or needs to reconvene because the data the participants needed weren't presented in a timely manner. Everyone in the room lost productivity because a key person was multitasking. My clients learn to set the tone of being present and not multitasking during their meetings, and they consistently report that their meetings end earlier, and result in better decisions, because everyone is engaged.

Always "On"

It's become the norm to surf the web while watching TV, text in the middle of a meal, or check Facebook while working on a deliverable. Although the need for constant stimulation is closely related to multitasking, it's a phenomenon all its own. The availability of technology may appear to be the biggest source of stimulation we have as a society, but we can't blame our need for constant stimulation solely on the presence of technology.

In a series of eleven studies, University of Virginia psychologist

Timothy Wilson and his colleagues at Harvard University asked participants to spend six to fifteen minutes alone in an unadorned room with nothing to do but think, ponder, or daydream about anything they chose. They were given a choice to push a button to administer a shock and end their session if they so desired at any time during their stay in the room, and each participant was given a sample shock before the study began. The participants consistently reported they did not enjoy the study and would have far preferred to engage in external activities, such as listening to music or using a smartphone—or even to give themselves mild electric shocks—than to have been with their thoughts.

Wilson believes our affinity for technology might be a response to people's desire to always have something to do. He notes, "Broad surveys have shown that people generally prefer not to disengage from the world, and, when they do, they do not particularly enjoy it. Based on these surveys, Americans spent their time watching television, socializing, or reading, and actually spent little or no time 'relaxing or thinking.'"[2]

Everyone Loves an Extrovert

In the book *Quiet: The Power of Introverts in a World That Can't Stop Talking*, author Susan Cain articulates in detail how American society has become deeply fascinated by and ultimately favors those who are charismatic, vocal, and dominant—all qualities of extroverts. Extroverts are defined as people who gain their energy from being with others and don't mind (and in fact often enjoy) being the center of attention. On the other end of the spectrum are introverts, those who gain energy from being alone, quiet, and able to contemplate their own thoughts. Cain provides numerous examples of how society favors extroverts and how often we dismiss or downright don't hear the contributions of introverts.

I see this bias play out with many of my clients and the companies they work for. Some of my clients consider themselves introverts and are naturally more observant and curious. They ask a lot of questions, rather than make declarations. They can be perceived as lacking confidence or weak because they aren't the most vocal in the room and don't always sound confident right away. So when a decision needs to be made, the extroverts in the room tend to offer solutions, and, instead of slowing down to draw out others' opinions, or even stopping to clarify what they are solving for, the meeting leader takes the suggestion from the extrovert because the group "needs" to move forward and remain productive. The problem with this cycle is that the extrovert is approaching the solution from their vantage point and usually has only a piece of the solution. Because we're so oriented toward productivity and favor extroverts, companies are creating half-baked solutions that often create problems down the road.

Because extroverted behaviors are so widely accepted and rewarded, we are creating a lopsided society—one that favors decisiveness, talk, and charisma over reflection, awareness, and wisdom. Extroverted behavior isn't bad by any means, but, like any strength, it has a shadow side or an ineffective element. When we believe that standing out and being heard are inherently more important than listening to and learning about others' perspective, we create a very self-centered culture. We confuse the natural power of extroverts, and in an attempt to replicate it we behave in narcissistic and self-indulgent ways.

An obvious example of this pattern is the recent emergence of Facebook, Twitter, and Instagram, as well as other social media companies. The instant and public nature of these sites only continues to reinforce people's need to get "noticed" by the external world in order to feel valuable, important, and loved. When I was on Facebook recently, I saw a young woman post that she liked her own Instagram picture just so she could get to twenty-five "likes," because that number made her feel good. When we continue to reinforce and reward looking externally of ourselves for an instant "hit" of worth, it will never, ever be enough. Ultimately, we will create a society where narcissism is the norm and self-awareness and inward inquiry are obsolete.

Our Brain Is Conditioned to Be on Autopilot

Another explanation for why we are biased to be on autopilot is that our brains are set up that way. The human species has evolved over centuries and continues to do so, and as we continue to evolve, our brain wiring and physical bodies are doing their best to adapt to our evolving environments. The body is an amazing system that does nearly all of its functioning on an unconscious level, meaning we don't have to "remember" or "think" about digesting our food or pumping blood to our hearts. Our bodies are incredibly adaptable and have their own inherent intelligence.

I once heard a neuroscientist speaking about the power of the mind-body connection, and he said he would rather be put in the cockpit of a fighter jet and told to fly without any training than to be in charge of keeping a human liver in balance. If we knew the intricacies of our physical system, I bet we, too, would be intimidated.

When our sense of survival is threatened, every part of our system is built to survive. Yet those very survival tendencies, when left unexamined, can be the source of reactive behaviors that erode our effectiveness and satisfaction with life.

Survival and Control

We are primal beings by nature, and our brains are wired to survive first, thrive second. This primal urge was the source of our survival as a species and is still an important part of our brain wiring. A relatively simplistic view of the brain, as it relates to survival and control, holds that our limbic system, located in the middle of the brain, "combines higher mental functions and primitive emotion into a single system often referred to as the emotional nervous system."[3]

The limbic system controls basic emotions, such as fear, pleasure, anger, and arousal, as well as the creation of short-term and long-term memory. It is made up of four important systems that work together, including the hypothalamus, amygdala, thalamus, and hippocampus. These four parts ultimately drive our survival response, also known as the "fight or flight" response, as well as our unconscious motivations (reward, pleasure, avoidance of pain) and emotional responses.

Although it's commonly thought that the amygdala is responsible for the fight-or-flight response (I even referenced this notion in my first book), it's important to know that our fear response is far more intricate and cannot be reduced to only one part of the brain. For our purposes here, though, I will refer to the unconscious, survival-oriented part of our brain as the limbic system.

LIMBIC SYSTEM—THE "EMOTIONAL BRAIN"

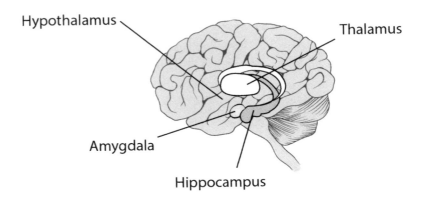

Hypothalamus

Thalamus

Amygdala

Hippocampus

With all parts working together, the limbic system operates automatically and incredibly fast. The limbic system is the automatic part of the brain that is constantly scanning the environment for potential danger and threat. Its main purpose is first to keep you alive, safe, and protected, both physically and emotionally. As information from the outside world comes in, it is first filtered unconsciously through your limbic system.

When your limbic system determines that something you are experiencing or are going to experience is a threat, it activates your body's natural stress response, which includes an increase in blood volume, rise in blood pressure, increase in glucose, and release of a hormone called cortisol to help you move fast physically. This is called the sympathetic nervous system, and it's designed to get us out of danger quickly without our having to think about it. This part of our brain is helpful when we are faced with physical danger. Our brain's ability to quickly take action without "thinking" has historically been imperative to our survival as a species.

Although our survival response isn't all of who we are, it's important to know that this primal part of the brain system still has a deep impact on our daily lives. As we have evolved as a species, the limbic system has evolved as well. Originally, humans operated from a simple mentality: "eat or be eaten." Now, however, the human species is not in as much immediate physical danger and our limbic system is on the lookout for twenty-first-century threats, such as emotional pain and loss of social status. Our limbic system is scanning all situations we are in to see if they could be embarrassing or painful or make us look bad. The way the limbic system determines whether something is a social threat is by constantly scanning our environment for potential pain and using our past experiences as a gauge.

For example, when I first started my business, it was stressful for me to balance my books, read my profit-and-loss statement, and put together proposals—pretty much anything involving numbers immediately triggered my fear response. No matter how much I tried to convince myself everything was fine and I could do it, my physical system didn't buy it. My limbic system was triggered based on my emotional memories of being a child who didn't feel smart, especially in math. I later found out that my confusion in math was because of a mild case of dyslexia. No matter the reason, if you've had a bad or painful experience, your limbic system's job is to remember it and then try to avoid the discomfort in the future. My emotional trigger around money and numbers might always be there, but that doesn't mean I'm at its mercy. I will walk you through how to work with your survival response in Part 2, but for now it's important that you know about how this unconscious part of your brain operates.

Mind Wandering

One of my clients was telling me about a conference he attended where he practiced being "present in the moment." He thought being in the moment would be easier, since he was away from his day-to-day activity and stressors and had the opportunity to sit and absorb information he was excited to learn. He admitted to me that as he practiced being present and really paying attention, he noticed almost every five to ten minutes that his mind would start to wander. He was frustrated with himself, because being present was important to him. I assured him that our brains are wired to wander, that in fact most people spend roughly 50 percent of their awake life engaged in mind wandering,[4] and that the first step to deepening presence is observing the experience of the moment. So the fact that my client observed his experience was a great step toward being more present. I encouraged him to keep observing his experience and quality of attention without judging himself.

Being present first is simply to notice, not to judge. My client wasn't going to be perfect, and neither will you. A lot of variables and conditioning are involved in our quality of attention, and shifting it won't and shouldn't be a quick turnaround.

When we are not focused on a specific task, our brains switch to what scientists call the Default Mode Network, a network of brain regions that are active when we are not engaged in a task and the brain is engaged in wakeful rest. According to R.L. Bucker in an Annals of the New York Academy of Science 2008 study, the Default Mode Network generates its own stimulation, such as daydreams, as well as thoughts about the future and the past. The preponderance of evidence suggests that the Default Mode Network is there to help us explore our inner experiences. The research further suggests that we do this so we can have a better idea of what is going to happen in the future—we think about things that have happened, we think about things that we hope might happen, and we use that information to help us anticipate what will happen in the future and to know how to act when it does.

Mind wandering is not bad; in fact, Eric Klinger, professor of psychology at the University of Minnesota, says, "We think of daydreams as scatterbrained and unfocused, but one of the functions of daydreaming is to keep your life's agenda in front of you; it reminds you of what's coming up, it rehearses new situations, plans the future, and scans past experiences so you can learn from them." Other benefits to mind wandering include the fact that most of our creative and innovative ideas occur when we are in the Default Mode Network. If you are constantly and actively making decisions about what to do next, you don't have space or time to activate your Default Mode Network, and you are less likely to have the type of aha moments gleaned during mind wandering.

Mind wandering is a natural part of our brain wiring and can both serve our creativity and detract from our ability to deeply rest, focus, and be present. The great news is that recent developments in the field of neuroplasticity are proving that our brain wiring is malleable—with training, we can develop new neuroconnections that enhance both creativity and focus.

We Are Wired to Avoid Emotional Discomfort

Another reason we have a bias toward not dropping in is that being in our head and "thinking" often feels far safer and more controllable than feeling emotions and sensations. Our brains are wired with a negativity bias, in which negative experiences stick to us as if we were made of Velcro and positive experiences roll off us as if we were made of Teflon. We are built to adapt and make the most out of painful, uncomfortable, and even unsafe environments, yet once we're physically and emotionally safe, that very protection mechanism can remain intact and cut us off from important information and experiences.

Early Life Conditioning

To understand the nature of early life conditioning, you have to consider that when we come into the world as infants, we are entirely dependent on our caretakers for our survival. We learn at a very early age what we need to do to stay part of our "tribe" so we won't get abandoned or hurt. Depending on the severity of the situation, you may have unconsciously learned that you needed to project happiness or humor to keep your parents happy, or that you needed to get certain grades or accomplishments in order to receive approval. Or you may have learned how to cook and feed yourself or your siblings because someone wasn't around to do it for you.

The brilliance of our psychological makeup is that we are wired to survive and thrive. Even if our childhood was dismal, our psychological systems have a way of making the best of the situation and creating productive behaviors to compensate for what we were experiencing. Because our nervous systems are so underdeveloped at this time, we learn without much thought at all about what's required of us in order to create a sense of belonging, safety, and security.

This is the nature of our early life conditioning—to come into the world and quickly react and learn what it takes to survive. Our reactive behaviors are unconscious and become our "operating system" for a good portion of our lives—unless we decide to examine our conditioning. Becoming aware of our past conditioning may be some of the hardest psychological work we can do but ultimately is the most freeing. When we begin to examine our conditioning and ultimately unhinge ourselves from it, we get closer and closer to our natural state of presence. Almost all of Chapter 3 will dive into our conditioning and how it shows up in our everyday life, while Part 2 is dedicated to how to work with our conditioned patterns.

Avoiding Pain

I suspect you can easily identify someone in your life who you would say is "in denial" in one way or another—meaning that person is working hard to avoid the reality of their situation in an attempt not to experience pain, discomfort, or loss. Robert Augustus Masters, author of *Spiritual Bypassing: When Spirituality Disconnects Us from What Really Matters*, explains that "part of the reason for this is that we tend not to have very much tolerance, either personally or collectively, for facing, entering, and working through our pain, strongly preferring pain-numbing 'solutions,' regardless of how much suffering such 'remedies' may catalyze."

When my colleague Jim lost his mother to cancer, his wife told me he seemed to be handling it pretty well. Although she said he had been working a lot more recently, that was because he had a big presentation coming up. Yet, several weeks after the presentation was over, he was still working long hours, regularly missed dinner, and didn't make it home in time to see his kids before bed very often. His wife became increasingly more frustrated, his kids were complaining, and when anyone brought it up to him, he fiercely defended how much pressure he was under at work.

After about three months, his wife had a serious conversation about the impact his long work hours were having on the family. She said, "Do you think this might have anything to do with your mom passing away?" At first, he blew it off and she remained silent. Eventually, Jim became very quiet, and his wife saw tears roll down his face. He looked up at her and said, "I think so."

Later, when I talked to Jim about the situation, he told me he had *honestly* thought it was just a busy time at work and hadn't drawn the conclusion that he was avoiding anything. When he justified his behavior to his wife and kids, he really believed what he was telling them was the truth. He told me it was a little scary because he was so convinced he was right and they were wrong. That's what is so pervasive about being on autopilot and our psychological bias toward avoiding pain. Our psychological system can be incredibly convincing, telling us we're okay and keeping us distracted, when what we're really doing is avoiding potentially painful emotions.

Instant Gratification

Not only do we naturally avoid painful experiences, but we also have a tendency to like instant gratification and quick fixes. Bottom line: we like to feel good and don't like to feel bad. That's how our minds are wired and conditioned, so when we do feel bad, such as by experiencing feelings of depression, anger, pain, or fear, we look for something that will "fix" it very quickly. We want it to go away, and we'll do just about anything to feel better.

Just take a look at the self-help section of a bookstore, and you'll see how oriented we are to quick, formulaic fixes to complex issues. The self-help industry is an $11 billion industry, and its most popular products promise a "seven-step solution" or "ten days to happiness" or a "success recipe." Such products are big hits because our society is so accustomed to everything being fast or instant. Our propensity for speedy solutions is evident in everything from fast food to instant videos to grocery-delivery services promising same-day dropoff. So, when we couple our avoidance of pain with our need for instant gratification, it's no wonder that we're being marketed and sold products all the time that help us avoid discomfort.

Yet even in a world where we have instant access to almost anything, we are still experiencing record levels of depression and stress-related illnesses and spending record amounts on sleep aids, antidepressants, and antianxiety medications.[5] In fact, one out of every ten Americans over the age of twelve takes antidepressants, and cases of depression in the United States rose 400 percent between 1988 and 1994. These statistics point to a dissatisfaction with the experience of life that is unconsciously being perpetuated and reinforced through the collective illusion that avoiding pain and looking for quick fixes is the solution to our dis-ease.

Summing Up Autopilot

Today, my face is *almost* as it was before October 2009, but everything else about me has changed profoundly. Since I healed from Bell's palsy, I have studied with multiple teachers about whole-body intelligence; the psychology of change; Carl Jung's teachings on ego, archetypes, and shadows; and with several nondual-wisdom teachers about mindfulness, presence, and awareness.

After having navigated my own wake-up call and having seen how much transformation occurs when we drop in, I feel even more passionate about the work that I'm doing around deepening awareness and presence. I see more and more the ways in which people are on autopilot, striving to do too much, stuck in their heads, and then not of service to anyone. In fact, being on autopilot gives us the opposite impact we desire and often unintentionally negatively affects our coworkers, employees, family members, and friends.

Moving away from the bias of the rational and conditioned mind is a little bit like being salmon swimming upstream—the odds are stacked against us. As depressing as all of this may appear, it is part of the reality we're living in right now. Another part of our reality is that, even in the midst of the biological and social forces at play, many of us have another, mysterious force propelling us to "wake up."

I feel optimistic about our hunger to collectively wake up from our state of autopilot. I'm encouraged by how many leaders want to engage in deeper, braver conversations about their own inner awareness. I'm encouraged by how many times the room has been filled beyond capacity when I've spoken to companies about presence. Something far greater than our rational minds is coming online, and we are at the forefront of a major shift in both personal and collective awareness.

We are hungry for clarity, well-being, and stability in this chaotic world, and the same inkling that prompted you to pick up this book is the energy that will spur you along in your own development and in remembering presence and awareness.

CHAPTER 2—Being Present:

A New Foundation of Awareness

I exist as I am, that is enough. —*Walt Whitman*

MOST OF US HAVE LIVED the majority of our lives in a state of autopilot, operating predominantly from our heads, with varying levels of effectiveness. At some point, we may become aware that we're living from this space and that, as a result, our options for anything else seem limited. Autopilot, or living in an unconscious state, exists as a survival and efficiency mechanism. It's helped humans to stay alive and conserve brainpower.

Dr. John Welwood, author of *Toward a Psychology of Awakening*, explains in his Sounds True interview "Healing the Core Wound of the Heart" that at the time of birth, humans are the least developed mammals on the planet. When other mammals are born, their brains and nervous systems are developed enough to enable them to walk within hours; they are therefore less dependent on their caretakers than human infants are. One of the reason humans are born underdeveloped is so we can fit through the birth canal.

The downside to being born this way is that our nervous systems are incredibly delicate and we are completely dependent on our parents or caregivers to keep us alive. Even for babies with the best upbringing and home environment, the nervous system goes into shock in the days, months, and years after birth. The newborn nervous system is physically, psychologically, and emotionally unable to process their experiences for many decades.

Rather, when children experience varying levels of confusion, pain, and trauma simply by being alive, their nervous system "freezes" those experiences in their bodies. If you think about it, it's quite brilliant that our systems' primary survival mechanism is to "store" our experiences until we are mature and safe enough to process them—although, according to Welwood, our nervous systems aren't mature enough to do so until we're in our forties, fifties, and sometimes even sixties. It's only when we have enough distance, stability, and sense of safety that we can go back and metabolize the experiences we unconsciously put "on hold" in our childhood. This perspective makes it clear that staying on autopilot can take only you so far. But what happens when simply surviving isn't satisfying (or effective) anymore?

When my clients become aware that they have been operating on autopilot, they usually begin to question how they would live their lives in a state of presence. What would it be like not to be so reactive? What would their relationships look like if they weren't at the mercy of their emotions? What would their experience of parenting be like if they weren't just going through the motions of getting their kids from one place to another? What would their level of connection with themselves be if their minds weren't spinning all the time?

When I tell my clients that they could evolve from being on autopilot to living from presence, they are intrigued, though they often aren't sure what that means or how they would do it. I explain to them that when we're living in a state of presence, we have a deep awareness of what is really going on in a given situation, so we start seeing things with an astounding level of clarity. I explain that they could live from a place of deep connection with themselves on all levels—mentally, emotionally, and spiritually—so they won't always feel as if external circumstances are whipping them around. I tell them they could know in their gut that they no longer need to feel compelled to prove their worth to anyone, ever. As a result, they can access a new, higher of level of vitality and contentment.

Before I start working with a new client, I like to discuss their motivation for deepening their level of awareness and presence. I remember a discussion with a potential client who told me, after I'd explained that this process of looking inward isn't for the faint of heart and that it requires a sincere commitment, "This seems like a lot of work." He stopped, seeming to contemplate what was before us, and asked, "Why would I do this?"

I could relate. I'd felt that way early in my journey. Why stir the pot if life is working relatively well? Why actively dive into the unknown when work feels "good enough"? These are very important questions to explore. You need to be clear on why you would explore a new way of being, as your "why" will be an important aspect of sustaining you through the process of deepening your presence.

Some people are motivated to wake up because autopilot is no longer working for them. Suddenly, their tried-and-true tactics for achieving "success" are not as effective as they once were. One of my clients, Debbie, told me in our first session that she took great pride in doing "whatever it took" to get her job done, including losing sleep, skipping meals, and skirting time with her family. Six months prior, she had been put on a major project at work. She confessed to me during our work together that no matter how hard she worked, it wasn't enough. She was no longer getting the results she was used to. Her kids and husband were complaining about never seeing her, she had been diagnosed with chronic fatigue syndrome, and she was at an all-time low mentally, emotionally, and spiritually. Debbie's strategies of skipping self-care and family time and ignoring her overall health weren't working this time around. She was confused, disoriented, and panicked that her life was falling apart—and on some level, it was.

Debbie may be an extreme example of what can happen, but the "crisis" she was in was what helped her wake up from her old patterns and explore a new way of living. Unfortunately, Debbie's experience is also incredibly common. For many of us walking around on autopilot, it often takes a significant wake-up call to direct us to reflect inwardly. What's important to remember is that no matter how intense the wake-up call is, the invitation is to reorient ourselves to a new foundation of awareness and presence and free ourselves from the conditioned patterns we've relied on for so long.

Perhaps you can relate to the experience of an old pattern no longer working as smoothly as it once did. Maybe the success of your external life is perfectly satisfying, yet you're experiencing an internal inkling for something "more." For me, after my Bell's palsy got my attention and I made some initial shifts in my life and practice of presence, my motivation shifted, too. Instead of being motivated not to get sick again or have a relapse, I became motivated by something more subtle and internal. This drive inside me was a deep, quiet, ever-so-subtle nudge to keep exploring. It was, and continues to be, an internal pull that draws me to a deeper level of presence.

After working with many people over the years around being more present, I have learned not to assess the timing of how, when, or even if someone chooses to become more present in their life. The truth is that I can't convince anyone, nor do I want to convince anyone, to become more present. The desire has to come from something within you—as a longing for, or an inkling that there is, something else available to you. What lies ahead of you is an opportunity to explore a new version of reality. Only you will know if or when the timing is right for you.

What Is Presence?

Presence is not something that resides or originates in your head, and that's why your mind has a heck of a time understanding it. Think back to your last great vacation. Can you recall a specific experience when you felt grounded and present? You might remember vividly the temperature, what the air felt like, the sounds and sights—remember how you *felt*. Now, imagine trying to explain that feeling of fullness and vitality to someone who wasn't there. It sort of loses its luster, doesn't it? The person you're talking to will likely be able to imagine your trip and even be happy for you (or envious), but they won't be able to feel it like you did. The best they can do is relate because they've had a similar experience.

This happens because being present is more than just a concept in your mind. When you're present—which can happen on vacation, because you finally allow the trappings of your day-to-day life to fall away—you experience things with all of your senses, beyond what only your mind can perceive.

When I was first learning about presence, I found the concept intriguing and exciting. My teacher at the time lived in Kona, Hawaii, and I went there to spend a week immersed in my own growth and learning. In preparation, I typed up all my questions about presence and e-mailed them to my teacher in advance. My questions were things like "How do you get present?" "Can anyone do it?" and "How do I teach it?" Once I got there, I sat down with my teacher for what I expected to be my first "official" learning session. I eagerly asked her if she'd received my questions. She said yes and then was silent. With much earnestness, I whipped out my printed list and said, "Okay, so my first question is—"

She interrupted me and said, "Let's head to the beach."

On the drive there, I was confused, excited, and a little nervous at the same time. I thought I was going to be learning from her—and now we were going to the beach? When we arrived, we sat on the sand for about an hour in silence. The entire time, my mind was spinning. I thought, "I spent a lot of money on this retreat. If I had wanted to go to the beach, I could have done that on my own." This was nice and all, but when were we getting the real stuff? The whole time we were on the beach, I was so preoccupied with analyzing, dissecting, and trying to "get" something that I completely missed the fact that my teacher was giving me an opportunity to drop in.

When I couldn't stand it any longer, I finally asked, with a distinct tone of desperation, "So, what about my questions?"

She replied, "You can't learn about presence from your mind, which is where your questions came from. Presence is about *remembering* something you already know instinctually."

I wanted to yell, *Then why the hell did I spend the money and time to be here with you?* Luckily, I kept that comment inside my head, but at the same time I felt frustrated and confused. I badly wanted a formula, instructions, or a recipe to follow, and she flat-out wasn't giving that to me.

What I now know, many years removed from that experience, is that my teacher sensed that my initial hunger for learning was coming from my mind's need to control. My mind wanted answers so it could feel safer in a situation that was confusing and disorienting. As a result of my disorientation and fear, my conditioned mind was trying to come up with all sorts of reasons why I shouldn't be there, or why it was a waste of time and money. Luckily, I trusted her because of our prior work together, and, looking back on it, I now see she was essentially exhausting my mind's chatter and allowing it to have its tantrum. She knew my mind would eventually give up trying to control the situation, and it did. My learning from there on out consisted mostly of experiencing presence, versus talking conceptually about it.

Presence is hard to explain, because it's something you experience viscerally, and that's what I learned on my first trip to Hawaii. I was so used to accomplishing, striving, and doing that when asked to "be," I became anxious and frustrated because I felt more comfortable "doing." Doing was something my mind could lock onto and something I'd been rewarded for my whole life. I know firsthand how hard it is to move from compulsively doing to resting into experiencing the moment. I didn't get to a place of deep presence on my first try. I stuck with it and continued to inquire about my conditioning and learned patterns that made it harder to sense presence. Every time I had the courage to explore more deeply, I experienced a more profound sense of rest, ease, and presence. Bottom line: presence is first and foremost an experience of being that can and will permeate your entire being.

Present-Moment Awareness

One of the easiest ways to access presence is to experiment with present-moment awareness. This means tuning into all of the richness and subtleties of the moment you are *in*, rather than thinking about moments in the past or the future. I know this sounds incredibly simple, but, as you might already know, tuning into present-moment awareness is not easy.

Since we operate on autopilot most of the time, it's easy to miss the details of the present moment. Can you remember the details of your last drive home? Can you remember the flavors of your last meal, or the emotional subtleties of your last conversation? Tuning into present-moment awareness itself can be life-altering because you're bringing conscious awareness to what you are thinking, feeling, and doing. Instead of missing the details of the moment, you can see and feel them at deeper levels. Present-moment awareness is life-altering, not only because you are setting yourself up for the chance to experience the wholeness that the moment has to offer, but also because you will begin to see your own and others' behavior with more clarity than ever before.

My client Joe had been actively experimenting with being more present both at work and at home. One strategy that helped him stay present was attending meetings with nothing in his hands other than a pad of paper and a pen. This was a radical, old-school decision, given that he worked for a technology company. After a week of experimenting with attending meetings technology-free, he said, "I cannot believe how much I was missing before." Joe explained that when he had previously attended meetings with his tablet or phone, his attention went to e-mails and the next urgent issue sitting in his inbox often triggered his mind to spin. He told me that now, instead of being distracted by something he couldn't do anything about (since he was physically in the meeting), he was able to give his full attention to the topic being discussed. He reported that, much to his surprise, he had a lot to offer, where previously he'd believed some topics irrelevant to him. He also noted how he could pick up on subtle body language from others and how that prompted him to ask about other people's perspective. He couldn't believe how much information he was gleaning simply by giving his full attention to the present moment. Joe ended our session by saying, "It's like, before I worked with you, I didn't know I had a vision problem, and you came along and gave me glasses. Now I can see everything more clearly."

When we're on autopilot, we don't see the situations we're in clearly. How could we? During the last ten years, I have observed hundreds of meetings, and I can say for sure that most of the people I've witnessed in those meetings were operating on autopilot, not in a state of present-moment awareness. I have seen the inefficiencies and costs of autopilot, including redoing conversations (because someone wasn't listening), emotional reactivity (because someone made an assumption based on past experience), rework (because all people weren't clear on the decision), and confusion (because many people were "checked out"). I could go on and on about the costs of autopilot, but I suspect you have experienced them firsthand.

The costs of the lack of present-moment awareness may be obvious, but the benefits may not be so much. In my last book, *Get Present*, I wrote in detail about the "benefits of presence," such as ease, efficiency, precision, creativity, and a sense of connectedness to yourself and your loved ones. These are benefits, for sure, but as I have deepened my own experience of presence, I've seen how they are actually side effects of returning to your natural state.

Although I see and experience many benefits of present-moment awareness, it is important to know that it doesn't necessarily ensure that you will have a peaceful life, void of frustration and pain. In fact, being fully present in the moment can and often does evoke a new level of awareness, and you may not enjoy what you're becoming aware of. Your practice of presence may reveal situations for what they actually *are*, versus what you want or hope them to be.

It's not unusual for my clients to experience an initial "honeymoon" phase with being present as they start feeling and seeing things more clearly. That first level of awareness is most certainly powerful and energizing. But the honeymoon phase can fade as they start realizing how few people around them are fully present. They attend a meeting, and no one makes eye contact or listens to each other. They sit down for a conversation, and the person they're meeting with is distracted. Or they go out to eat and see how many people are on their devices, rather than engaging with one another. Their new level of clarity highlights the reality of our culture and can evoke a range of emotions, from frustration to loneliness, anger, and even despair.

As clients deepen their understanding of presence, they express that the beauty of presence is that the external events of their life— good or bad—no longer take them on a ride of emotional ups and downs. They have access to a sense of internal stability that eluded them before. They report that the life events that took them off center no longer impact them in the same way. They feel more rooted, connected, and even guided in every aspect of their lives. Again, it's not that they are experiencing bliss or happiness all the time; rather, they have a sense of well-being and abiding awareness that is far deeper, more reliable, and more stable than any fleeting emotion.

Present-moment awareness is a state of being, and the next sections of this chapter are designed to guide you through a few different entry points to experiment with how to cultivate this awareness. I consider it a win if anyone can strengthen their awareness of the present moment, because that means they have moved beyond autopilot and entered into a new and foundational awareness that will support them the rest of their lives. In the words of one of the readers of *Get Present*, "It doesn't feel like I'm trying to do much differently, but I can't help noticing more, and that alone has been worth the time I put into reading your book."

Experimenting with Present-Moment Awareness

The beauty of experimenting with present-moment awareness is that you can try it anytime and anywhere. The goal of experimenting is to increase the quality of your attention and observation in any given moment. When you acknowledge presence, you are no longer on autopilot. The moment you bring your attention to and observe fully where you are, what you're doing, what you're thinking, feeling, or experiencing, you have left the world of unconsciousness and entered the world of presence. Our days, months, and years are made up of moments—one right after the other—so there are countless opportunities to explore present-moment awareness.

As with any new habit or practice, you will remember to be present, and then you'll forget. Then you'll remember and forget again, and so on. Every time you remember to be fully present in the moment, you are changing your brain's wiring and your entire system's makeup. If the path in your brain is used to being mostly on the autopilot superhighway (unconscious thought and behavior), it makes sense that blazing a new trail in your brain will take a little while. I work with a lot of overachievers, and I often need to remind them that presence is not about getting it "all right, right now." Have some compassion and patience with yourself as you start. Remember, every time you bring your attention to the present moment—no matter what you're doing—you've jumped the track of autopilot to the new track of conscious awareness. When you jump the tracks enough, you will have created a new super highway and way of relating to your entire world!

It's important to understand that experimenting with present-moment awareness may bring up some triggers. In other words, your mind will have some things to say about being present. In fact, almost as soon as you notice a sensation or experience in the moment, your mind will want to judge, assess, understand or otherwise categorize it. That's what our conditioned minds do. We are all conditioned—and wired—to make assessments of our experience, but when we judge what we're experiencing, we have left the present moment. I'll get into the brain science behind our conditioned reactions in Chapter 3, but for now the invitation is to experiment with deepening presence without judgment.

Body Awareness

Your physical body can be one of the most effective and precise tools to help you tune into awareness of the present moment. The challenge with tuning into body awareness is that some of us are so in our heads that awareness of body sensation can easily elude us. One of my clients said it best when she admitted that she thought the purpose of her body was to hold her head in place. She was blown away when she figured out that her entire body was packed with powerful information to help her process her experience of the present moment.

Since what we're going for is a deepened awareness of presence, tuning into any sensation you are experiencing is a step toward it. Since you reside in your body every moment of the day, you have a lot of opportunities to tune into what it is experiencing. The following ideas are intended to help you notice physical sensation for the purpose of tuning into the present moment. Remember, the key is not to judge your experience but simply to acknowledge it.

- When walking, notice how your feet hit the ground or how they feel.
- Notice the temperature or smell of the air when you're walking outside.
- Pay attention to how your clothes feel on your body.
- When washing your hands, pay attention to how the water and soap feel on your hands.
- When eating, notice the texture, flavor, and temperature of the food.
- Move your neck side to side and pay attention to the sensation.
- Experiment with the quality and speed of your breath; notice how far into your belly it goes, and see if you can slow it down and deepen it.

- Place the tip of your tongue right behind your front teeth and relax your jaw.
- Lift your shoulders up, hold for five to ten seconds, and then release them.
- The next time you are exercising, bring more attention to the details of your experience (e.g., your foot placement, arm movement, breathing).
- While standing in line, notice the placement of your weight. Is it forward or more on the left or right? Can you feel your feet on the ground?
- When driving, notice the sensation of your hands on the steering wheel.

These are just the tip of the iceberg in terms of opportunities to tune into your body sensation as a way of strengthening your awareness of the present moment. You can be aware of body sensation anytime, anywhere, so the next time you're bored in a meeting, standing in line, or sitting in a waiting room, leverage that time to tune into your body sensations and deepen your experience of presence.

Another powerful tool to tune into the present moment through the body is a body scan, designed to methodically bring your attention to different parts of your body and simply to cause you to notice what is occurring in that section of your body in the moment. I will walk you through a body scan here, but note that it's difficult to do a body scan and read at the same time, so I invite you to read this section a couple of times to get a feel for it, then take yourself though the practice mentally or have someone read this section aloud to you. I also offer a free recording of this body scan on my website: www.yaoconsulting.com/whole leadership corner/resources

Body Scan

Note: The body scan can take as little or as much time as you desire. I like to do a daily scan that takes about five minutes, and then other days I spend twenty to thirty minutes diving deeply into the experience. During any part of this scan, you may experience emotions or thoughts arising, and that's perfectly normal. Your job is simply to notice them, not to assess or make judgments about your experience. Your anchor (always) is your breath, so whenever a sensation or experience begins to feel overwhelming or too difficult, bring your attention back to your breath. Also, the body scan process is mostly about practicing being present in the moment, so try not to worry about "getting it right." If you're noticing more than you were before you did the body scan, you're on the right track.

Find a comfortable to place to sit with your feet on the ground and your spine supported and upright. Close your eyes or turn your gaze down toward the ground. Bring your attention to the sensation of your breath. Notice how far your breath goes into your belly, or if you mostly feel your breath in your chest, notice that. Don't make a judgment about how deep your breath goes; again, this experience is about noticing and observing your experience in this moment. Take three more natural breaths, paying attention to the quality and depth of the breath in your chest and belly.

Bring your attention to your head and notice if there is any tension. Focus behind your eyes, then the back of your head, and then your jaw. What sensations do you feel? Bring your attention to any spot where you feel tension, and take a couple of conscious breaths. When you are ready, bring your attention to your neck. Move your head side to side to help you notice the sensation. When you feel any pain or tightness, don't judge it or try to make it go away. Simply bring your attention and deepened breath to that spot. It may shift, or it may not. Either way is okay.

Bring your attention to your shoulders. Tune into the position of your shoulders. Are they tense or shrugged? See if you can relax them and bring them away from your ears. Take two deep breaths while paying attention to the sensation of your shoulders. When you're ready, move to your chest and specifically to your heart. Pay attention to how your heartbeat feels. Is there tightness in your chest? If so, again, no need to judge it. Simply bring your breath to your chest and heart. Notice if the sensation changes when you simply bring your awareness to the tension.

Now bring your attention to your solar plexus (the area right below your chest and above your lower abdomen) and abdomen. Take another deep breath and see if you can bring your breath a bit more deeply into this area of your body. Take another nice, slow breath as you bring your attention here, and remember that your job is simply to notice what you are experiencing.

Bring your attention to your tailbone and hips. Move your hips and the base of your spine from side to side to help you tune into the sensation of this area of your body. Bring your attention to your sits bones. When seated, is the weight of your body evenly distributed between the right and left sides? What sensation do you experience when you bring your attention to this area of your body? Take another deep breath.

Then bring your attention to your legs and feet. Can you feel all the way down to your feet? Tune into the solidness of the ground under your feet. Take a breath and simply notice any sensation that is presenting itself now.

Bring your attention to any other part of your body that is requiring your attention now. Spend as long as you'd like paying attention to the sensation. When you feel complete, take three slow and conscious breaths. Wiggle your fingers and toes to help bring you back to the present moment, and when you are ready, open your eyes.

Our physical bodies are chock-full of information about how we are doing, our stress level and even how we feel emotionally about any given situation. Our culture is not taught to tune into our bodies for information, but the more you practice tuning into body sensation, the more you will likely learn about yourself and your experience of the present moment.

Awareness of Thoughts

One of the most common experiences people have when they start practicing present-moment awareness is that they become acutely aware of just how much mind chatter is occurring in their heads. In fact, many people don't enjoy the experience of tuning into the present moment (at first), because when they do, they realize how much their mind is spinning, thinking, analyzing—all the time.

One of my friends and I were discussing meditation, and she said she didn't like it because she wasn't "good" at it. When I asked what she meant, she said, "Every time I sit down to meditate, I can't get my mind to settle down, so I just end up getting more stressed out because of all the things my mind is thinking about." One of the biggest misunderstandings I see with people starting to experiment with meditation or tuning into the present moment is that they think they should have a clear and quiet mind. The reality of tuning into the present moment is that it's likely your mind will be anything but quiet—and that is perfectly okay. I speak in detail about noticing the content of the mind in the "Interlude" section, but for now, know that quieting your mind is *not* the goal in acknowledging present-moment awareness.

The purpose of tuning into the present moment is simply to tune into what's going on in your mind, not to try to change it. When my friend asked me, "What do I do when my mind is so busy? How do I get it to calm down?" I said, "Nothing." There's nothing to do except notice. That's the brilliance of presence. About a year later, she told me that my simple answer—to do nothing—had been incredibly freeing for her. She no longer felt like she was meditating "the wrong way" when she had a busy mind. She also explained that she had noticed her experience of tuning into the present moment was different each time she did it, and that sometimes it was peaceful, sometimes her mind was really active, and sometimes she just felt the sensations in her body. Of course, her experiences were different each time, because the moment she was in was different.

It's important to keep in mind that if you are not familiar with tuning into presence, you might feel as if you are at the mercy of your spinning mind, and I know personally that is not a fun experience. You don't have to get on the merry-go-round of your mind; in fact, the more you realize your spinning mind just comes with the territory of our stressful twenty-first-century lives, the more you might feel empowered to relate to it differently.

When my clients become more aware of their daily thoughts, they are usually overwhelmed and annoyed by the incessant chatter. Have you ever truly paid attention to what your mind is saying at any given point in the day? If we had to sit next to a person who said out loud all the things our minds say to us during a thirty-minute period, we might think we were sitting next to someone insane! Mind chatter itself has qualities of insanity, as the thoughts are often random, judgmental, disjointed, repetitive, unhelpful, and not rooted in present-moment reality.

Our minds are conditioned to comment on, judge, assess, and evaluate all of our experiences, so mind chatter is something we can't do away with, but when we know mind chatter is part of the experience of life, we can bring some perspective to it. Unfortunately, when we're operating on autopilot, it's easy to identify with myriad thoughts and get taken on a mental or emotional ride. When we're on autopilot, we don't stop to observe or question our thoughts and we get caught in the thought, versus simply being aware of it.

When we have looping thoughts, and when we think the same thoughts over and over again, those thoughts become habitual. When your mind is looping, you are strengthening the neuropathway for the thoughts. The more you do that, the more it reinforces the same thoughts, again and again, until they become so ingrained that they happen "automatically."

Joe Dispenza, author of *You Are the Placebo*, says that "we have anywhere from sixty thousand to seventy thousand thoughts in one day, and 90 percent of those thoughts are exactly the same ones we had the day before."[6] The only way we can shift our thinking, emotional responses, and behaviors is to bring consciousness to them. The only way to bring consciousness to our habitual thinking is to practice present-moment awareness so we have some space to start questioning the validity and helpfulness of our thoughts.

When my clients are practicing becoming more conscious of their thoughts, I ask them to keep track of their most repetitive thoughts for one week. This exercise is what I call a "twofer," not only because they learn more about their unconscious thoughts but also because the exercise sets up present-moment awareness, as it's not possible to do this exercise without being present. Logistically, I ask my clients to get a notebook and reflect on as many thoughts as they can for that day. After a few days, they start to see a pattern in their thoughts. At that point, they are to identify the three to five most prevalent thoughts that arise for them. For example, one client wrote down these four predominant thoughts:

- I don't have enough time to complete my work.
- I'm behind.
- My boss is going to scrutinize this.
- I'm not good at this.

These thoughts were all driving her to work longer hours than she wanted to. When we met to discuss her list, I asked her not to assume these thoughts were accurate and instead to inquire about the validity and impacts of these thoughts from an objective perspective. I first learned about this process of examining thoughts from a friend and colleague who had attended a weekend event with author and coach Byron Katie. With a slight adaptation from Byron's process, I guided my client to use this inquiry with each of her thoughts. I suggested she ask herself:

1. Is this thought true?
2. Is this thought helpful?
3. Is this thought necessary?

She was surprised to discover not only how often she had these thoughts, but also how unhelpful they really were once we asked these questions. She had the hardest time with her thought of feeling behind. She told me that it felt absolutely true that she was behind on her project and it was difficult to move past that. When I asked her if the thought was helpful and necessary, she could easily have answered no. When I asked her to inquire about how the thought of "being behind" impacted her, she told me it paralyzed her. Once she felt behind, her mind started thinking about all the things that would happen if she didn't get her project done, and then her stress level spiked, resulting in her not eating well and staying up late, spinning her wheels, which only put her further behind on her project.

When we identify and believe the thoughts we're having, or, worse yet, don't have awareness of our thoughts, we will forever be at the mercy of our busy (and sometimes insane) minds. The only way off the runaway thought train is through present-moment awareness.

Awareness of Emotions

Through the process of the body scan, or really any process of tuning into the present moment, we open ourselves to deeper levels of awareness. When I take groups through the body scan process, a few participants inevitably stumble upon emotions they weren't consciously aware of stored within their bodies. When I asked one particular corporate group to share their experiences after the body scan, one woman raised her hand and said, "I was perfectly fine before I did the body scan, and now I feel like crap." I inquired a bit further, and she explained that she felt a pain in her shoulder that "wasn't there before" and that she'd come out of the experience feeling sad and tired.

I listened with curiosity and compassion because she was clearly agitated and frustrated, but I also reminded the woman that we didn't "do" anything except turn our attention inward. It's not as if the five minutes of deepening awareness "created" her pain in her shoulder, her exhaustion, or her sadness. Those were there the whole time; she had been operating on autopilot and didn't have awareness of what was going on for her internally. I also reminded her that the only thing that happened was that she became *aware* of her experience. The great news, I told her, was that she was now aware of what she was working with. She now had information that she was tired, sad, and in pain. Autopilot was giving her a false sense that everything was okay, but the truth was that everything was not okay for this woman. Because she tuned into the present moment, she now had a fighting chance to make choices to address her physical and emotional pain.

Everyone experiences varying levels of pain, trauma, disappointment, betrayal, grief, and a host of other painful emotions throughout their life. As a collective culture, we are not well trained on how to express and metabolize those painful emotions in healthy ways. What we are wired and conditioned to do is ignore, stuff, deny, reject, and despise uncomfortable emotions. When we do this, however, it's not as if those emotions suddenly "go away" (as much as we might think or hope they do). Rather, those unprocessed emotions get stuck and stored in our physical bodies.

Each emotion possesses a certain kind of energy or frequency. I like to think about emotions as "energy in motion." When we don't deny or avoid our emotions, they move, are metabolized, and clear out of our system organically. When my clients come upon uncomfortable emotions in our sessions, I guide them not to judge or evaluate the experience of the emotion, but rather first to breathe and simply be with the experience of the emotion. An emotion, even an old, painful one that's been stuck for some time, can clear quickly if you stay very present to the experience of the emotion arising. I discuss working with emotions in Chapter 5, but, depending on the intensity of the emotion, you may want to find additional support in guiding you through processing your emotional experience.

I'm the mother of two school-age boys, and I work diligently to help them tune into their bodies and emotions so they can process them and get them out of their systems. For years, as a family, we have talked about the concept of feelings "getting stuck" in our bodies and how much better we feel when we let them out. When my oldest son was eleven, he was having a rough time in school. For a couple of weeks he was mopey and quick to react emotionally, and it was tough to connect with him. His moodiness wasn't the standard preteen angst, either; I sensed it was something different.

I trusted that an opportunity to address it with him would present itself, and it did. I came upstairs during a weekend day when we didn't have much going on. I was puttering in the linen closet outside his room and caught a glimpse of him facedown on his bed. I asked if I could come in, and I sat down, saying nothing. After a few minutes of just being with him, I said, "Honey, I get the feeling that something isn't quite right for you. You seem sad." He shrugged his shoulders and didn't say anything. I asked him if he would be willing to tune into his body. He agreed, and, since this wasn't a new conversation, he was familiar with what I was asking and also with what he normally feels like. I asked if he noticed anything in his body, and he pointed to his chest and said, "It's in here."

I put my hand on his chest and encouraged him to breathe into the tightness there. I breathed with him. Then I asked, "What do you need, honey?"

With much clarity, he said, "I need to cry."

I said, "Well, go for it. Let's get this out of your body."

He cried hard for about two minutes, although it felt like a lot longer because it was so intense. After the initial wave subsided, I asked him to tune back into his chest and asked again what he needed. He said, "I need to cry again."

The second wave was even more intense than the first, and all I could do was support him by breathing and being a loving presence as the emotion was clearing his system. After the second wave passed, we sat quietly for a while, and then I asked him again what he needed. He told me he wanted to be alone for a bit, and I gave him a kiss on the head and left the room. After about thirty minutes, he came downstairs and looked visibly lighter. As the day progressed, he was naturally more conversational and started playing with his brother, and I heard him laugh for the first time in a couple of weeks.

The beauty of doing this work with children is that they usually don't have much of an interest in or need to create a mental story about the stuck emotion, or a desire to figure out what is happening on an intellectual level. My son had enough experiences of tuning into his body and releasing emotion that this experience was no different than any other time he had done it. My son and I sometimes talk about this experience of his letting go of emotion, and now he practices a body scan on his own when he's feeling stressed or down. We can all get important information from our bodies and help clear stuck emotion if we tune into presence and the intelligence of our bodies.

Present-moment awareness is the antidote to being on autopilot. As long as we're on autopilot, we will not be able to see our experiences with clarity. When we don't see our experiences with clarity, we are unable to make empowered choices about how to shift our physical, mental, or emotional experience. Although you may not like what you see as you initially become more present, you will at least be informed about the reality you are in. In my experience, present-moment awareness and the clarity that comes from it is the single best place you can start to truly transform your experience of life.

CHAPTER 3—The Presence Tug-of-War

You must unlearn what you have learned. —Yoda

AFTER MY BELL'S PALSY EXPERIENCE, I actively started experimenting with a deeper level of presence. I enjoyed the experience of being present, and I naturally wanted to know how to be present all the time. Anyone who engages in deepening their presence can attest that being present isn't as easy as flipping a switch. In the initial stages of my presence journey, I was frustrated by how often I "forgot" and returned to a state of autopilot. Then something would cause me to "remember" to be present again. Sometimes I would return to presence because I was experiencing discomfort of some sort, and other times remembering presence would happen spontaneously, without a rational explanation. Either way, my experience of presence felt like a light switch—on, then off, then on again—and I couldn't figure out why this switching back and forth occurred so often. A client of mine, Scott, referred to this forgetting-remembering experience as a tug-of-war. He described it as a part of him pulling him toward presence, while another part of him was pulling him toward his old patterns and behaviors.

As you begin to drop in or deepen your experience of dropping in, the tug-of-war between autopilot and presence will feel real and at times quite challenging. No matter the level of your intention and commitment, you will flip between autopilot and present-moment awareness, sometimes without even being aware of it. You will not sustain present-moment awareness 100 percent of the time, and that "goal" will likely only cause you frustration. In fact, there's a different goal altogether when it comes to practicing present-moment awareness, and that is to notice the tug-of-war and pay attention to what triggers that push-pull and ultimately causes you to forget presence. This is a practice of strengthening your ability to be present, rather than being perfect.

Deepening our ability to tune into the present moment is challenging because of the physiological makeup of our brain, as well as our past conditioning. This chapter focuses on giving you context about the main reasons why we are in a presence tug-of-war and, of course, what we can do about it.

Safety in the Status Quo

In Chapter 1, we talked about the limbic system, the survival-oriented and emotional part of the brain. This part of the brain system is unconscious, meaning we are not aware that it is always scanning our environment for threats and storing emotional memories.

When you are faced with an uncertain, new, scary, or potentially painful situation, this part of your brain will activate. I suspect you can think back to a situation when you felt nervous and your heartbeat was racing. When this happens, it becomes hard to take a deep breath, and you can feel your adrenaline pumping. That response is actually helpful when you need to get out of danger quickly, but the problem is that our nervous systems are so amped up from the constant stimulation of our daily lives that we end up living most of our lives based on an unconscious survival response.

Beyond what I consider the obvious relational, social, and heath challenges stemming from living in an adrenalized state, one of the other biggest issues that stems from operating primarily in an unconscious and reactive state is that it keeps us in the status quo of our lives. One of the primary focuses of your limbic system is to keep you safe, and it is easier to do that when you stick with your habits and predictable routines, essentially remaining on autopilot. For your survival brain, predictability equates with safety. This is why even the thought of doing something new can sometimes trigger a fear response.

The limbic system uses your conditioning—all of your past experiences—to determine whether something you are experiencing is a threat. Your conditioning includes direct experiences, like thought, emotion, and memories, as well as the belief systems you were taught, such as religious, political, and, social beliefs.

Everyone's conditioning is different, which is why when two or more people are exposed to the same situation, some of them will be triggered, while others won't, based on their conditioning. Your limbic system uses your past experiences to determine whether what you are experiencing in the moment is "safe" or not. When we look at our current experience through the lens of our past conditioning, we have no chance of seeing the situation with clarity and therefore are unable to respond productively.

I hear people refer to their conditioning as if it's something they cannot change or just have to "deal with." Specifically, one of my clients referred to her conditioning as her "emotional baggage," while another one said, "That's just my personality," to explain away a behavior she was getting critical feedback about. It's normal for people to build a part of their identity from their past conditioning. But it's important to know that your conditioning is something you picked up along the way, or that was layered upon you throughout the course of your life. It's not "who" you are. You came into this world as a fully present being not run by your thoughts. You came in aware, observing and noticing your world, and experienced your new environment through your senses. Everything you have gained and lost through your life experience is part of your conditioning, and in order to return to or remember your natural state of presence, you need to develop a relationship with your past conditioning—meaning, you need to be willing to examine, explore, and question your conditioned or autopilot responses.

Moving Beyond the Status Quo

If you're reading this book, I suspect you're not the type of person who gravitates toward maintaining the status quo. You like to expand, learn new things, and take risks, and you know there is more to life than just surviving. The part of your brain that thinks rationally, that's willing to take risks and try new things, is located in the prefrontal cortex, or frontal lobe.

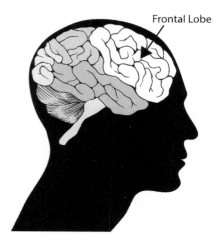

Frontal Lobe or Pre-Frontal Cortex

Your frontal lobe is the executive-functioning part of your brain, responsible for expressing language, impulse control, objectivity, empathy, humor, flexibility, judgment, and complex problem solving. When you use this more sophisticated part of your brain, you are able to assess danger and threats with more clarity, not from a place of past emotional experience, which is what your limbic system does. The responses of your limbic system are not very sophisticated. They are more like the responses of a child who hasn't learned about life yet. Your frontal lobe's responses are more like those of a mature adult who has had a lot of life experience and uses those experiences and skills to make effective decisions, including how and when to take risks. For the purposes of simplifying language, I will refer to our survival response and limbic system as the "low mind" and the frontal lobe as the "high mind," keeping in mind that the sophistication and complexity of responses from the limbic system are narrow and limited, while the responses of the frontal lobe are robust and intricate.

When you engage in something new, or attempt to expand your skill set or knowledge base by choice, or consciously decide to expand beyond your autopilot pattern, your low mind will likely get triggered and your body will respond accordingly. Remember, the low mind relies on the status quo to keep you safe, so this tug-of-war my client noticed as he was waking up from autopilot is actually a push-pull between the low mind and the high mind. With consistent and directed attention to the relationship between the low mind and the high mind, we can move beyond the status quo more easily.

Neuroplasticity is the brain's ability to create new neuropathways. It was once believed that our brains became cement-like and unalterable after childhood. However, recent science has proved that our brains are malleable and adaptable, more like plastic. The great news is that, with focused and consistent attention, we are not "stuck" with our old, reactive conditioning. In fact, we can self-direct shifts in our brain circuitry. We will talk more about self-directed neuroplasticity in Part 2, but the great news is that we are not at the mercy of our low mind.

The Reactive State

John was a senior manager who was feeling challenged to move beyond his compulsion to attend every meeting he was invited to. When I asked him why he wanted to look at this particular issue, his attendance at meetings, he told me he always felt behind, had no time to work on the issues that were coming up in meetings, and sensed that he could be leveraging his time in a more effective way if he wasn't always in meetings. On the flip side, he felt he shouldn't miss any meeting, even if getting there required extraordinary measures. He was traveling a ton to attend various meetings, and that was causing problems at home. He didn't particularly like to travel but believed he had no choice.

John could articulate that the mere thought of not attending a meeting he was invited to triggered his low mind. He told me when he looked at a meeting request on his calendar and saw that it conflicted with other things on his schedule, the realization that he couldn't be in both places caused him anxiety. Through our work together, John had enough present-moment awareness to be acutely aware of the body sensations of his triggered state, including shortness of breath, a faster heart rate, and what he described as "sheer panic." He shared that he knew objectively that if he skipped or missed a meeting, everything would be okay. He knew that he could send one of his employees and that he really wouldn't miss anything. He said, "I know I'll be fine, but it still freaks me out."

What John was describing was the visceral feeling of the tug-of-war between his low mind and his high mind. He knew that staying focused on his breathing and presence would assist the emotional reaction in subsiding, and it did within about twenty minutes.

In helping John process his triggered state, we worked to see if we could identify the origins of why he reacted so strongly to the idea of missing a meeting, especially in light of his objective knowledge that no harm would come to him if he reprioritized how he used his time. Using a technique I learned during my Leadership Circle certification program, I asked John, "If you were to miss this meeting, what would that mean?"

He quickly said, "Nothing. I would send someone in my absence, so I know it would be totally fine."

I told him that what he had just told me came from the "adult," objective part of his brain (his frontal lobe or high mind), and that that was not where the reactivity was coming from. I asked him to specifically tune into the emotional experience of missing a meeting and asked him, "What would it mean if you missed a meeting?"

In a much quieter voice, he said, "It would mean that people would notice I wasn't there."

I asked, "So, what would it mean if people noticed you weren't there?"

He responded, "It would mean they would think I'm not working hard."

"What would it mean if people thought you didn't work hard?" I asked. My line of questioning kept guiding him more deeply into the emotional experience of what it would mean to miss a meeting. Every once in a while, John responded from "logic," whereupon I gently reminded him to stay with the *emotional* experience, since that was the source of the reactivity.

John ultimately identified a particular belief that if he missed a meeting, it might lead people to think that he didn't care about them, or that their needs weren't important to him, and that would result in their being disappointed in him. I asked him what that would mean, and he shared that if people were disappointed in him, he felt as if they would think poorly of him, and that would eventually lead to his losing his job, his family, and anyone who loved him.

"Can you think of another time when you felt scared that if you didn't do what people wanted, you would lose their love?" I asked.

John's was gazing at the floor quietly; then he looked at me and said, "Yeah, that was pretty much how I felt with my parents." He went on to explain that he thought of his parents' attention and love as conditional, and that he believed in order to keep their love, he had to do exactly what they wanted and not disappoint them. He told me he distinctly remembered having disappointed his parents and what a "horrible feeling" that was. John had grown up believing that disappointing people was not an option. He had formed this assumption early on in his life and had never deeply examined it.

Following the breadcrumbs of John's thoughts and emotions led us to a deeply rooted emotional memory of his having to "be good" in order to be loved and accepted. When I said to John, "Okay, just to recap, you believe that if you miss a meeting, it could eventually lead to the loss of everyone and everything you love? Is that right?"

John immediately burst into laughter at how ridiculous that sounded, but he agreed that was right. I felt deep compassion for John in this moment because, on an unconscious level, he had been carrying around this belief for more than forty years. It made perfect sense, given his associations, that his low mind would be afraid of missing a meeting and that it was simply trying to protect him from experiencing the emotional pain of rejection or abandonment.

The brilliance of the low mind is that its orientation toward survival is incredibly generative when we need it the most. As a child, John was conditioned to be compliant and to maintain his parents' approval. His compliance propelled him to do very well in school and opened doors to top universities, and because he did so well in college, it opened doors to great career opportunities, and so on. John's conditioning not to disappoint people set him up for a very "successful" external life. The better he did in school, the more praise and approval he received and the "safer" he felt. However, through this experience of reflection, John was starting to realize his conditioned behavior was no longer helpful because it had created so much tension internally. He told me that the more praise he received, the more he sought it out and "needed" it. He even called himself an "approval addict." John was incredibly motivated to examine his conditioned reaction because his addiction to approval was not only causing him a lot of stress but also frustrating his wife.

When John was promoted to senior manager, he was immediately thrown into situations where he could not please everyone. In an attempt to keep people happy, he traveled more than he needed to, regularly stayed late at work, and put his personal life on the back burner. He told me that his wife was so mad at him for over-committing, in an attempt to keep other people happy, that she was at a breaking point. And John could not keep everyone happy, so his reactive pattern was no longer helpful or generative.

When John reflected on his complying tendency, he realized how his past emotional experience of having disappointed his parents was so intense that his low mind was unconsciously driving his behavior in attempt to avoid experiencing the pain again. Through John's reflection on his past, he had traced the emotional pattern that his low mind was using to drive his unconscious behavior. With this knowledge, John had a fighting chance to look at his compulsive overfunctioning at work and consciously shift his behavior. (In Part 2, we will dive into working with conditioned patterns, but for now the important thing is to see that the reactive nature of your low mind is not "bad." In fact, it often is very helpful when it's needed, although eventually you no longer need it.)

Over time, we simply outgrow the conditioned pattern that helped us when we were younger. These types of patterns are no longer generative and eventually start backfiring and even create the very thing we don't want. John's low mind didn't want him to experience the pain of not pleasing people, but ultimately he caused frustration for the one person in his life who was closest to him: his wife.

Once we can identify our unconscious triggers and conditioned behaviors, we then have the opportunity to objectively see a given situation for what it is, rather than what our low mind perceives it to be through the lens of our past emotional experience. John's ability to understand the origins of his trigger allowed him to operate from his high mind, which gave him a better opportunity to make conscious and objective choices.

After a few months with his newfound clarity, John gleefully reported that he canceled several "not so important" business trips so that he could be at home more and connect with his wife in a more meaningful way. He also told me his employees had been excited to step up in his place and to have an opportunity to expand their visibility and gain more experience. The icing on the cake was when John said, "I feel like I'm not working as hard as I did before, and I'm not as afraid to say no or set boundaries now."

The Three Reactive Tendencies

Karen Horney, psychoanalyst and author of *Our Inner Conflicts*, has had a great impact on our understanding of human behavior. She has identified three fundamental character structures or styles of relating to which we default by the time we reach adulthood. Her theory states that the behavior patterns to which we default are based on our unique childhood experiences. We learn to behave or react in ways that will create the greatest sense of safety and belonging, given our external circumstances. Horney's work references the three main relating styles as:[7]

- *moving toward* people (compliance)
- *moving against* people (protection)
- *moving away* from people (controlling)

Robert J. Anderson and William A. Adams, authors of *Mastering Leadership* and cofounders of the Leadership Circle, use Horney's relational styles to further define three basic reactive tendencies to which most humans default in one way or another by the time they reach adulthood. These three reactive tendencies are compliance, protection, and control.[8]

Compliance tendency: The reactive tendency of compliance is rooted in the underlying assumption that in order to be safe and loved, you need to "be good" or submit to others' authority and control. Compliance behavior is characterized by giving away your power in order to be liked, included, or approved of. Compliance behavior is oriented toward maintaining relationships over anything else. This reactive tendency values relationships and lack of conflict.

Examples of compliance behavior include:
- Giving up, even when you have strong opinions
- Avoiding conflict
- Overworking in order to prove oneself
- Failing to initiate tough conversations
- Having a deep desire to keep others happy
- Being unable to set or maintain boundaries
- Going along with ideas you don't agree with
- Being unable to articulate your own vision or needs
- Quietly disagreeing with decisions
- Feeling powerless

- Resenting other people's control/authority over you
- Acting passive

Remembering that our reactive tendencies were helpful at one point in our lives is important. Because we're discussing the unconscious nature of our conditioned patterns, the rational mind might be quick to evaluate reactive tendencies as "bad." Be aware that we are not vilifying or making your reactive tendencies wrong. Rather, we are examining your conditioned response and consciously choosing which behaviors are now most helpful, given where you are in your development process as an adult. Although we are talking about how to move through our conditioned response so we can be at choice about our response, it's important to remember that each of the reactive tendencies also possesses fundamentally valuable gifts.

The gifts rooted in the compliance tendency include:
- Loyalty
- Recognizing needs in others
- Love for self and others
- Willingness to be of service
- Building community
- Championing values
- Preserving heritage

My client John, whose story we read about above, was conditioned to be a good kid and follow the rules his parents set for him. He was conditioned to work for external rewards, and early on he associated approval with a sense of safety and worth. John's story is an example of how the reactive tendency of compliance can express itself.

Protection tendency: The reactive tendency of protection is rooted in the underlying assumption that in order to be safe and create a sense of worth, you need to create and maintain distance from other people. Protection behavior is characterized by being emotionally removed and/or intellectually "superior." Protection behavior emphasizes self-interest over engagement with others. This reactive tendency values rationality and critical thinking.

Examples of protective behavior include:
- Approaching issues intellectually, void of emotion
- Blaming
- Acting superior
- Acting defensive, including by placing blame and fault finding
- Withdrawing or shutting down
- Being overly critical or rigid
- Appearing aloof, cold, or inhumane
- Relying exclusively on rational thought and data
- Excluding oneself from discussion or debate
- Taking pride in one's independence
- Seeing what's wrong first
- Dismissing or criticizing ideas from others

The gifts rooted in the protection tendency include:
- Inquisitiveness
- Challenging others' thinking
- Discernment through detachment
- Strength of character
- Mentoring others to own their ideas
- Offering wisdom
- Adopting a wider perspective
- Caring deeply for a few people or causes

When I first met Gina, it was in passing, when her manager stopped her in the hallway to introduce me to her. Gina barely made eye contact with me and came across as aloof and cold. Gina's apparent lack of interest in our meeting made me feel dismissed and unimportant at first, but by doing my own internal work, I knew enough not to take anything too personally and instead absorbed our first interaction as "data" for if or when we began to work together. Based on my initial experience with Gina, I sensed she might be expressing the reactive tendency of protection.

In my first session with Gina, she seemed different than she had during our first interaction. She asked good questions and had incredible insights about the organization's culture. She came across as inquisitive and introspective. When I asked her why she was interested in leadership coaching, she said, "I feel misunderstood." As our conversation deepened, I learned that Gina had a reputation for being aloof, intellectual, and cold. I could understand the perception, based on our first meeting in the hallway, and could also see why she felt misunderstood, because she was so different in this meeting. Gina went on to tell me that she received consistent feedback that she was argumentative in meetings, and that people found her difficult to work with because she always defending her ideas. Gina had hit a wall when it came to influencing others and couldn't figure out why people didn't adopt the strategies she offered. When I asked her what she thought was the real reason behind people's not adopting her ideas, she said, "Honestly, I think it's because they aren't that bright. I don't want to sound arrogant, but nine times out of ten, my strategies are the most sound."

After Gina and I worked together for a few weeks, I learned that her parents were both highly respected scholars who worked with PhD candidates. She shared that when she was growing up as an only child, it was common to have PhD candidates over for dinner, debating various academic concepts or current affairs. She told me she tried to participate in the conversations, and, with the guidance and support of the students and her parents, she learned to express her views with conviction and objectivity. She was rewarded (with praise) when she could effectively engage in whatever debate was happening around the dinner table. She reflected on how she used to study up on current affairs or the subjects her parents were teaching just so she could keep up with the conversation. Additionally, when Gina wanted something from her parents, they encouraged her to "present and defend" her proposals. They evaluated not only the content of the proposal (such as a request to stay out later than her given curfew) but also her ability to defend her proposal. Gina's ability to remain emotionally detached and to quickly analyze other people's contributions and perspectives led Gina to be very successful in debate and eventually to earn a master's in business administration from Harvard.

Gina explained to me that she had very good memories of sitting at dinner, discussing "adult" topics, when she was a child. It made her feel a part of the group, important, and smart. Of course, there is nothing overtly wrong or traumatic about Gina's experience, but what happened there was that at a very young age, she (unconsciously) began to build an identity around her ability to be smart. Her ability to think analytically and precisely articulate her position served her well academically and set her up for a great career, but now that she was a senior leader, her identity as the smartest one in the room was backfiring. People who default to the reactive tendency of protection often pride themselves on maintaining separation from the group by being superior (usually at an intellectual level) and showing up as analytical and rational.

Controlling tendency: The reactive tendency of controlling is rooted in the underlying assumption that in order to be safe, you need to be self-reliant and that creating a sense of worth is all up to you. Controlling behavior is characterized by maintaining control in service of achieving external results. Controlling behavior values results and achievement over relationships.

Examples of a controlling tendency include:
- Talking over others or interrupting
- Bulldozing people into decisions and not bringing others along
- Taking charge in every situation
- Being a perfectionist
- Engaging in autocratic decision making
- Micromanaging
- Viewing most things as a competition
- Having unrealistic expectations of self and others
- Having low tolerance for mistakes and learning curves
- Believing "failure is not an option"
- Wanting to be the best

The gifts rooted in the controlling tendency are:
- Creating outstanding results
- Valuing continuous improvement
- Doing whatever it takes
- Being persistent
- Having personal energy
- Having high standards
- Possessing a strong ability to influence others
- Speaking out
- Excelling in most situations
- Working hard for what one wants

Another one of my clients, Pete, grew up with what he refers to as "hippie parents." They were constantly moving around, living at campsites, and his mom handmade all the family's clothes. Although his parents told him they were attempting to give him a "creative" and "organic" life, he mostly remembers not feeling stable, secure, or abundant as a child. He told me that he recalled sitting in the rain at a campsite, thinking, *When I grow up, I will never live like this.* That feeling propelled him into wanting a great education and job so he never had to feel the insecurity of not knowing what was coming next, as he did as a child.

This is exactly how our survival response serves us at an early age. Pete's low mind was imprinted with the uncomfortable experience of not feeling secure, and the motivation to avoid those feelings was enough to set him on a path to creating a sense of safety for himself. Without his parents pushing him, Pete figured out that when he worked hard at school, he performed better than everyone else, and that gave him a sense of worth. He learned to be self-motivated, eventually earned a scholarship to an Ivy League school, and is now a senior leader at a Fortune 100 company. He and his wife have lived in the same house for most of their marriage (well beneath their means), their two kids have both received a great education at prestigious schools, and he has created a life that most would describe as very successful.

In Pete's organization, it's expected that leaders change leadership roles every few years. When the time came for Pete start exploring new roles, he told me he was starting to lose sleep, working longer hours, and feeling easily triggered about things that he hadn't been triggered about in a long time. He also confessed that he was spending a lot of his time trying to find out the "scoop" about where he stood in the company, applying for jobs he didn't really want, and worrying about his family's spending. Even though Pete knew intellectually that he had enough money saved to live very comfortably for many years without working, he was still at the mercy of his unconscious reactivity, as his low mind had the emotional imprint of fear when it faced uncertainty. His controlling behavior became more obvious to his colleagues, and they started wondering what was going on with him. His manager eventually had to call Pete aside to discuss his combative behavior toward his coworkers and his overall sense of stress. Before Pete had begun looking for his new role, he had been known as a very positive and inspiring leader. But the unconscious trigger of the unknown of a new role caused his behavior to shift, and his controlling tendencies were creating stress and tension and eroding his reputation as a leader.

Each of the three reactive tendencies has innate gifts, and the point of examining our reactive tendencies is primarily to gain more awareness of what may be unconscious. Although I will not offer specific "tools" to work with each reactive tendency (as that is a robust enough concept and is beautifully articulated in Anderson and Adams's book, *Mastering Leadership*), all of Part 2 offers ways to work with your reactive tendency, no matter its specific flavor.

The Mind's Spell

The principal idea we're exploring in this chapter is that our conditioning is something we adopt unconsciously as a way to cope with and adapt to our experiences starting in our early years of development. When we begin to move beyond our conditioned patterns, it can feel as if we're taking two steps forward and one step back. With Pete, because he and I had been working together for a while and because I was familiar with his reactive tendency, it took only a few minutes for me to guide him to make the connection between his reactive and controlling behavior and his past conditioning. Once Pete acknowledged the connection, he said, "Dammit, I know this stuff—why do I keep falling back into my old pattern?" This is a common response when people are becoming aware of their reactive tendencies. There are moments of clarity where the person feels empowered to make choices about their behavior, and moments of not remembering and being at the mercy of their unconscious pattern. This is part of the development process, so don't be too hard on yourself if you witness this response coming up for you.

One of my clients, Nancy, told me after several of our sessions, "I feel so clear now. I wish I could feel that way when I'm not with you." I explained to her the reason she felt so clear was that our conversation helped her "wake up" from an unconscious state, in which her conditioned mind, or low mind, was running the show. When she shifted to a more present and conscious state, she told me she felt more vitality, clarity, and resourcefulness. The longer we worked together, the less she felt the stark difference between the "before session" and "after session" experiences. Over time she had become more familiar with her unconscious patterns and behaviors and understood the source of them, and it was easier for her to wake herself up from an unconscious state. Nancy enjoyed the clarity that came from her presence so much that she was willing to engage with uncomfortable emotions because she knew that was the fastest way to gain deeper clarity and a sense of vitality. She knew that the decisions she made from a deepened state of awareness were far more reliable than the ones she made from a reactive, unconscious state. For Nancy, the experience of presence was worth the discomfort of examining her conditioning.

One of the hard things about becoming more present is that it's not always tidy. Sometimes our experience of examining our conditioned responses can be painful or embarrassing, something we would prefer to ignore. But people hire me to help them become aware of thoughts, behaviors, and feelings that are unconscious. Even though our conversations aren't always something they "enjoy," per se, my clients consistently express a level of relief and appreciation when I help them remember their own presence.

Many wisdom teachers describe an unconscious state as a "dream state," an "illusion" or "trance." I like to think about the unconscious state as being under some sort of magical spell. It doesn't matter how you think about the reactive state—the point is that when you are unconscious, you don't really know what you're doing, why you're doing it, or even how you got there. You're operating solely at the whim of another force (in this case, your low mind). When you're at the mercy of your low mind, you have no choice in how you respond, because the entire process, from trigger to reaction, is unconscious.

Since I have two school-age sons, I've heard a lot about Harry Potter over the years and have watched most of the movies. I can't help but to see Harry's journey as a great example of our quest toward presence. During Harry's various quests, the antagonist inevitably attempts to stop him by putting him under some sort of spell. The spell usually causes Harry to "forget" about where he's going, why he's fighting, and who can help him. In every book, Harry has to work hard to remember his powers, wake up out of the spell, and continue toward fulfilling his true purpose. We're no different. Although our low mind isn't the antagonist of our life, it can sometimes feel that way. In fact, the survival part of our system is what is conditioned to keep us "safe" at all costs, even if keeping us "safe" comes at the expense of our expansion.

In general, most of my clients have some awareness they are stressed, moving too quickly, and operating from their heads. When I ask them about their choices, they usually say things like, "On some level, I know this stuff, but I just don't do it" or, "What you say makes sense, but I just don't have time." That is the spell talking. Part of us knows (our inner knowing) that something is off, but another part of us (the mind spell) tells us we don't have time, permission, the ability, and so on, to make a change. In fact, one of the signs of being under the "spell" is the feeling that you have no choice.

Believe it or not, when I hear these statements from a client, I get excited, because if they have enough awareness to voice that they know "better," that means they have enough consciousness to shift their behavior. So if you have ever had similar thoughts, consider yourself in a great place—a place where you have enough awareness to make a significant shift in your life.

The goal is not to ever fall asleep or ever to be under the spell but rather to be aware that you have fallen under the spell, and to work toward not staying as long, and to have the power to pull yourself out of it so you can continue on toward your true purpose.

A New Perspective

Everyone knows a child goes through important development stages from birth to adulthood, but rarely do we hear about the developmental stages of adulthood. It makes sense for children's behavior to be reactive and unconscious. They are not capable of understanding or ready to understand the complexities of life, nor can they fully take care of themselves. But as adults, we've had the space and time to create our own lives and likely to have our basic survival needs met. Therefore, not only are we developmentally ready to become conscious of what was once unconscious, but it's an imperative part of our growth as adults that we do.

We have an opportunity to move beyond our past conditioning and to uncover our true nature and potential. When we come into awareness of our deeply embedded and unconscious reactive tendencies, we actually enter into new life possibilities and experience a fundamental shift in the source and sense of our worth, identity, and safety.

This fundamental shift is simply an evolution or maturation process each of us has an opportunity to experience. We can shift from our unconscious reactive tendencies to a more authentic, aware, and creative expression. This evolutionary process is well documented in the stages of adult development, but, for the purpose of simplification, we'll turn to the language that Anderson and Adams, founders of the Leadership Circle, outline in their comprehensive leadership model. They explain that we, as grown adults, have the opportunity (and, I might say, the imperative) to expand beyond our reactive conditioned patterns (low mind) into what they call the creative or aware state (high mind).

When we engage in the evolutionary process of moving from reactive to creative/aware states, the shift occurs on mental, emotional, and even physiological levels.

Aspect of Self	Reactive	Creative/Aware
Primary brain function	Limbic system	Frontal lobe
Orientation to life	Safety: "play not to lose"	Purpose: "play on purpose"
Identity	External accomplishments	Internal experience
Behavior	Reactive/autopilot	Conscious/ resourceful
Mindset	Fixed	Growth
Motivated by	Fear/control/survival	Inspiration/vision/ creativity

Most adults have had some experience of questioning the purpose of their life. They ponder questions like "Is this all there is to life?" "What's my real passion?" or "Why am I working so hard?" Things like money, status, and titles may suddenly not satisfy them the way they used to. These kinds of questions sometimes arise for people spontaneously, or sometimes they're triggered by life-altering events, like the loss of a parent, friend, or job. No matter how or why this new perspective starts to emerge, it's an important and natural stage of your development. When my clients start to question their purpose or whether what they're striving toward matters as much as they once thought it did, it can be disorienting for their conditioned mind and in many ways threatening to the identity to which their mind has been oriented for decades. The newness of this natural inquiry can be scary for some, and often our first reaction to questioning the purpose of our life is to deny or resist the experience. We either don't fully acknowledge or try to deny the emergence of the spontaneous and natural unfolding that is occurring. The questioning itself is not a bad thing or something we should deny. Instead, view it as the initiation of the next phase of your evolution and maturation process.

When we allow our conditioned minds to identify and look outside us for a sense of worth, relevance, and strength, we will forever be chasing, searching, and unsatisfied. Building an identity based on accomplishments, material items, and status is a normal part of our maturation process, but it's not where our development should end. Too many people get stuck in an external orientation and resist the natural desire for deepened awareness that is trying to emerge. When my clients admit they are questioning their lives, feeling unsatisfied, or have "escape fantasies," they usually immediately follow those admissions by saying something like, "But those are just crazy thoughts. I have a mortgage and kids in school, and I just need to get my head back in the game and get focused." Perhaps you've had this same internal tug-of-war dialogue. But these "crazy" thoughts are actually a sign that the energy within you is naturally moving from a reactive state to a more creative/aware state. It's a natural life-force energy that is starting to awaken within you. It's not something to fear or resist, but rather something to notice and to inquire into. The point of this line of questioning is to make space for your creative energy to begin to express through you. Allowing for authentic, creative expression to emerge requires a dismantling of the conditioned patterns you developed in your early years. They simply are no longer needed for where you are in your life.

As a culture, we collectively have a hard time letting go of things we are attached to or have built. Terms like "disintegration," "falling away," and "breaking down" aren't popular, because our low minds conjure up feelings of anxiety, fear, loss, and pain—and who wants to go there willingly? Yet the truth about the adult maturation process is that it is quite liberating. It is the time in our lives where we have a chance to move beyond the trappings of our conditioning and have the opportunity to fully integrate the clarity, creativity, strength, and power that reside in our whole-body intelligence. We have the opportunity to examine and dismantle our conditioned patterns so we can expand beyond it and access the essence and power of who we naturally are.

However, your conditioned mind is not likely to perceive this expanded awareness as something "positive." If you think about it, moving beyond your conditioned pattern is an ending of sorts, and, as with any ending, it might be painful or scary. However, if you tune into your deeper awareness, the awareness beyond your conditioned mind, you might feel that there is another part of you that is very curious and quite willing to explore a new perspective on your life.

Author and teacher Cynthia Occelli articulates this process of maturing or moving beyond our conditioned state in the following quote: "For a seed to achieve its greatest expression, it must come completely undone. The shell cracks, its insides come out, and everything changes. To someone who doesn't understand growth, it would look like complete destruction."

I think about our past conditioning as our "shell"—a protective layer we needed to survive. There comes a time in our lives when we no longer need the protective nature of our shell, and when it in fact becomes quite restraining. So ensues the tug-of-war between the part of us that wants to remain the same and the part that wants to expand beyond the confines of our conditioning or protective "shell."

I suspect if you tune into your inner awareness right now, you might feel the inklings of the tug-of-war between your conditioned, low mind and your deeper knowing that there is something more, a more expansive way of being in the world. When you feel this sensation, try relying on presence to help you navigate your way through the tension. Our low mind, when faced with any ending or proactive shift in our consciousness, will automatically resist it. Because our low mind can't grasp the concept of "growth," it does not understand that voluntarily moving beyond our protective shell might be a positive thing. When you tune into presence, you can ground yourself by asking questions like "In this moment, am I okay?" "Am I safe right now?" "Am I at choice?" By asking yourself these questions, you create a bit of space between your thoughts and conditioned reactions. By creating space, you will have the opportunity to remind yourself that the essence of *you* and your reactions are two very different things.

Remaining rooted in presence brings you back to the reality of the situation at hand. This is a self-directed process, in which you are shifting from your old survival mindset and into exploring more creative and aware ways of relating to your world. For some, facing the option of examining their lives, their low mind panics, as if they are about to physically jump off a cliff. When you are in the present moment, you will understand that I'm not asking you to jump off a cliff. You will see that you are completely at choice about how you engage with awareness. You will find that you are not in a life-or-death situation (even though your low mind would like to convince you otherwise). Present-moment awareness can anchor you and help you to keep coming back to awareness and clarity when your low mind is reacting.

Part 1 Reflection

The first part of this book described the states of autopilot and presence and offered explanations about why we experience the tug-of-war between the two. Here are some important key points to remember from this section:

- We are facing massive influences from our culture, emotions, thoughts, and body that create a fog or spell that keeps us from being present.
- The limbic system (low mind) is designed to constantly and unconsciously scan our environment for threats and uses past emotional memories to determine whether something we're experiencing (or about to experience) is a threat.
- Conditioning is something we pick up along the way or that our past experiences layered upon us; it is not the entirety of our being.
- As a result of the family situation each of us grows up in, we all adopt reactive tendencies, such as complying, protecting, and controlling, that initially help us thrive.
- There is a natural point in our evolution or adult maturation where we have an opportunity to explore our reactive tendencies and conditioning and to decide what behaviors remain generative and which don't.
- Recognizing creative energy starting to emerge may

evoke more questions than answers at first, and may feel scary or unsafe to the low mind.

- The journey toward presence and moving beyond the status quo may be uncomfortable or new, but ultimately we can be liberated from our old, reactive and unconscious patterns.

Before you move on to the next section, take a few moments to pay close attention to any internal tension you may be feeling about engaging in exploring presence. Notice your low mind's commentary, and don't try to change it. Maybe take some time to write down what your experience of this book has been so far. Do you notice that you want more answers, or do you just want to move on? Do you feel resistant? Excited or inspired? Or even a little disoriented or overwhelmed? Whatever the experience, just notice it and don't judge it as good or bad. It's all just data about how your system is absorbing the information and the opportunity ahead.

It is important to keep reminding your low mind that you aren't getting rid of it, vilifying it, or making it wrong in any way. It likely gave you exactly what you needed to get you where you are now. Now, you are just exploring creative and aware options for how to relate to your life, giving yourself the possibility of a broader and more liberated experience.

Ideas or Reflections

Interlude—The Revealing

of Stable Ground

WE'VE SPENT THE FIRST HALF of this book diving into our conditioned patterns, the brain science behind our reactions, and the ways in which we are often culturally set up not to be aware of presence. The next half of the book is designed to help you rest into your natural state of presence and align with your clear mind, connected heart, and courageous gut. Then, from the solid ground of your whole being, we will explore how to relate to and work with your conditioned patterns.

Many of us live at the mercy of our thoughts or emotions and as a result feel a lack of stability or groundedness. What this means is that when an emotion or thought arises, we have the experience of having no choice but to be whipped around by the experience. As with a wave crashing over you and knocking you off your feet, being at the mercy of thoughts and emotions can be disorienting, surprising, and scary because you don't know if you will ever come up for air. Yet being taken over by thought and emotion is not your only choice.

Reflecting on the tenets, we know that each of us has a preexisting state of presence and stability that is always available. Once clients I'm working with experience presence, the next question they often have is "How can I access presence more often?" The question is natural and comes from a place of trying or wanting to get somewhere other than where they are. But what's not always obvious is that presence is available at all times, and the way to "find" it is not by actively trying to find it.

A foundational part of presence is the feeling of being grounded and stable. The way I learned to access the stability of presence was from Adyashanti, wisdom teacher and author of *Falling into Grace,* during his Art of Meditation class. My perception of the world was blown open when I learned that I had a choice about where to put my attention, and that I didn't have to be swept away by my thoughts or emotions.

Our thoughts, emotions, and sensations in any given moment are what Adyashanti calls "content." Other terms that describe content are "mind chatter," "monkey mind," and "ego." Content is the thoughts, emotions, and sensations that feel unstable, unpredictable, and consuming of our attention. Presence and stability cannot come from the content of our experience. Yet many of us place all of our attention on the content of our experience, not realizing there is any other option. Focusing our attention on a micropart of our experience is like walking into a beautiful garden and focusing only on a rock, not even realizing that if we shifted our attention, we would have an entirely different experience.

When we focus on a tiny portion of our experience, we miss the wholeness of it. We miss that outside our focused attention on the rock, there are trees, flowers, water, and a sense of spaciousness and awe. We have a choice about where to place our attention. Our awareness is often constricted to the content of experience, and what we want to do is turn attention to the awareness of the greater context. The content of experience is happening within a larger context. When I reference context, I mean the subtle, unchanging, constant energy that has no form, commentary, agenda, or judgment. The energy of context is that it simply "is." Other language for context is "source," "light," "consciousness," "silence," "essence," and "pure awareness." When we acknowledge the context of awareness, it can give us an immediate sense of connection, stability, and peace.

We can all acknowledge the awareness of the context of our being at any time, because it already exists, whether we're consciously aware of it or not. In our garden analogy, just because you are focusing on a rock doesn't mean you are not in the garden. In the image below, you can see that the content of your experience is only a small portion of experience at any given time, whereas the context of the experience is vast, expansive, and always present.

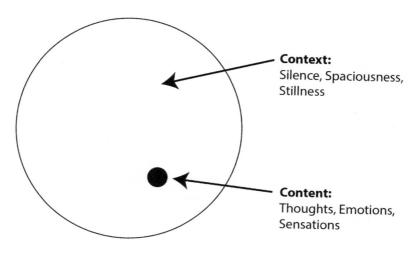

Context:
Silence, Spaciousness, Stillness

Content:
Thoughts, Emotions, Sensations

Turning our attention to the context of being is a radical shift in consciousness, and this is where you will access true stability. The stability and clarity we need to navigate our chaotic, unpredictable, and noisy world cannot and will not come from our mind or by focusing solely on the content of our experience.

When I first learned about the idea of content and context, I immediately had a vision of going up into space. Even though I have never been to space, I could imagine the feeling of lifting off the ground and seeing my home, my city, my country, and eventually the whole earth getting farther and farther away. I could see the earth as a whole, and for a moment I was just floating in the space and silence of the universe. A tremendous feeling of peace and deep "okay-ness" came over me, and I suddenly had a very different perspective, particularly about the importance (or lack thereof) of my ever-changing thoughts and emotions. I could see from the vantage point of floating in space that my thoughts and emotions were no different than the weather patterns on Earth—they just came and went, and I had no need or ability to control them.

Acknowledging the context of my being was incredibly helpful when I was dealing with the death of my father-in-law in February 2016. Although we anticipated his passing, it still came as a shock, and a whirlwind of activity quickly ensued. People's emotions were on edge, and we all had to make several tough and rapid decisions. Even in the midst of the grief and flurry of logistics, when I closed my eyes for even a few moments, I could drop into the visceral feeling of okay-ness and peace. Granted, I didn't stay there terribly long, because I had phone calls to make, but I could still feel it and know it was there, always. From that place of knowing and stability, I was able to navigate and support my family with deeper clarity and compassion.

I will keep coming back to this idea of content and context throughout the next part of this book, but for now, here are few important points to keep in mind:

- **You are not content.** The mind tends to build an identity based on thoughts and emotions, but do not mistake the content of your mind for who you are. The essence of who you are *is* the awareness beyond the mind. That doesn't mean we will try to get rid of the mind or change it; it just means don't mistake a small portion of your experience for all of who you are.

- **Choosing what to acknowledge.** Just because you are used to focusing on the content of experience doesn't mean you can't acknowledge the context at any time. Whatever you bring your attention to strengthens it, so I will keep inviting you to acknowledge the existing context of experience, rather than only the content.

- **No need to suppress any of your experience.** Turning attention to the context of your being doesn't mean you must suppress the content of your experience. Your mind and emotions will forever be active, and I'm not suggesting that you try to stop, eliminate, or even quiet them. Instead, turn your awareness to the preexisting silence and stillness that is the *container of the content.* From this vantage point, you will be able to be in relationship with your thoughts and emotions differently, and then the mental and emotional patterns will begin to unwind themselves.

- **Presence knows what it's doing.** Without any intervention whatsoever, presence and awareness know where to go, what to do, and how to navigate your varied experiences. Presence is an intelligence beyond your analytical mind that provides deep stability and guidance in moments of uncertainty and unknowing.

Similar to the tenets, these principles are not something I expect your analytical mind to fully comprehend or agree with. Instead of trying to understand these principles from the mind, allow them to simmer in your consciousness for a little while, and when you feel ready to move on, do so. I even invite you to be a bit liberated by the mystery of *not knowing* what they mean and to see how they reveal themselves to you throughout the rest of the book and in your life. As with everything I offer, please remember that ultimately this inward journey is yours and that you must investigate these principles on your own to see whether or how they are true for you.

PART 2—ACCESSING CLARITY, CONNECTION, AND COURAGE

Your past perpetuates itself through lack of presence. The quality of your consciousness at this moment is what shapes the future. —Eckhart Tolle

ALTHOUGH THERE IS NO "set" path for evolving from a reactive state to a clear, aware state, there are some predictable twists and turns in the road. This next part of this book is designed to help you deepen your awareness of your reactive patterns and guide you in how to relate to them and tune into your natural state of presence. All of us have patterns that are set up in our systems—anything from our morning routines to how we walk, talk, and think to how we respond to fear. Patterns in our thoughts, emotions, and even physical bodies are automatic and unconscious and often ingrained in our systems from an early age, so when we begin to work with them, we must be aware at every level of our system.

In the following chapters, I offer ways to work with our patterns by connecting to three distinct aspects of your being: clear mind, connected heart, and courageous gut. Although you will read them in a progressive way, it doesn't mean that working with your patterns or the content of your experience is a linear process. When you drop into deeper awareness of your mental patterns, it can spontaneously trigger your dropping into a deeper part of your system. For example, I was working with one of my clients, Sean, on examining his thought patterns, and it ended up triggering his emotions. Over the course of two sessions, we discussed where his reactive patterns had originated and how they were playing out for him at work.

Before his next scheduled session, he e-mailed to ask if we could have a quick phone call because he was upset. He told me that when he had visited his parents over the weekend, he had experienced his family dynamics differently than he had in the past, and that an unexpected wave of anger had come over him. He was concerned because the anger felt so "out of the blue" that it surprised him.

Before we dove into the nitty-gritty of Sean's emotional experience, I guided him in accessing his inner stability. We did this through a quick guided experience of acknowledging presence, and as a result he could "remember" the tenet that he is not his thoughts or emotions. Although his thoughts and emotions felt very intense, the content of his experience didn't have to dominate his experience. When Sean shifted his attention and acknowledged presence and awareness, he told me he felt immediate relief.

The purpose of tuning into presence was not for Sean to

avoid his thoughts and emotions, but rather to help him find stable ground first so he could examine his reactivity without getting swept away by his thoughts, stories, or emotions surrounding his family dynamics.

Only from the stable ground of presence could Sean begin to work with his family dynamics at both a psychological and an emotional (head and heart) level, and he eventually drew the connection between his family dynamics and his compulsion for perfectionism. Having this awareness of the origination of the pattern and its impact on his head and heart allowed Sean to consciously move away from his old patterns and make a choice about how he wanted to relate to his work (and life).

By turning his attention and awareness first to presence, then to his thought pattern, he was led to the next place that needed attention: his anger. Then he followed the breadcrumbs of awareness to the next place, and so on. Prior to Sean's family visit, he wasn't manufacturing or trying to work through his family dynamics, although he was aware of them. Instead, he paid attention to his awareness of his entire experience during this visit (not just his thoughts or emotions, but also the context of his experience), stayed with it and didn't try to suppress or change the experience, and allowed it all to unfold. Through our presence alone, we are led to clarity and ultimately to the opportunity to be liberated from the grip of our patterns. As we relax into awareness and presence, the patterns begin to unwind.

The idea of awareness itself beginning to unwind your conditioned patterns may feel counterlogical, especially because most of us are conditioned to believe that if we want something, we have to "do" something to make it happen. The primary "doing" on your part will come from remaining connected to presence. After that, awareness and presence know what they're doing. They will guide you to the next place for you to engage. Throughout the following chapters, I will offer several concrete tools and experiments to enable you to work with your conditioned patterns, but keep in mind that acknowledging awareness and presence, the context of your being, is the single most important and effective thing you can do.

CHAPTER 4—Accessing the Clear Mind

Remember one thing: meditation means awareness.
Whatsoever you do with awareness is meditation.
—Osho

THE FIRST STEP IN ACCESSING the clear mind is to disentangle ourselves from thinking our thoughts are who we are and, instead, to (always) shift our awareness to the stable ground or context of our being. This concept alone is radical for many people because we are so wrapped up in the content of our minds that it never dawns on us that we aren't what we think. Until you learn that you are not your thoughts and see them for what they are—a temporary experience—they will dominate your life, for better or for worse.

When we begin to drop in and explore the distinction between the content of our mind (thoughts) and the context of our being (preexisting stillness, calm, and awareness), it can feel like opening up a junk drawer: it's often jam-packed, you don't know what you're going to find, and the thought of cleaning it out can be overwhelming. As with our experience with a junk drawer, it's common for our first reaction to the apparent messiness of our inner world to be a desire to make the mess go away somehow. We may want to just dump everything in the trash or quickly shut the drawer. Either way, the conditioned mind will want to control the experience.

The hallmark of dropping in is that you aren't controlling anything. In fact, the very notion of control is contrived. As a recovering control freak, I sometimes find it amusing that letting go of control is something I write and teach about. But I have learned that the more you try to control your mind and try to make it "clear," the less clear it will be. If you've ever tried to make a thought go away, I suspect you know that effort can be very difficult, and that the thought rarely stays away forever. It's sort of like holding a beach ball under water: you can do it for some time, but it takes a lot of energy, and if you become distracted or lose balance, the ball shoots wildly to the surface and sometimes hits you (or someone else) in the face. In an effort to move away from "control or avoid" techniques, this chapter will guide you in how to be in relationship with your thoughts. Instead of trying to suppress them, change them, or judge them, you will learn that bringing awareness to your thought patterns is all you need to be liberated from them.

I'm a huge fan of allowing everything I do to come from flow or ease, and although seeing my thoughts for what they are—just more content—was new and unfamiliar to me at first, I have found tremendous ease in no longer being at the mercy of my thoughts and mental patterns, and in finding an internal stability I didn't know existed.

In a clear-minded state, you can see situations for what they are, as opposed to viewing situations through the lens of your past conditioning. You can accurately decipher where to take responsibility and where not to take things personally. You can also discern when and how to navigate new terrain, even if it feels risky. This chapter gives you context and tools to help you create space for the clear mind to emerge and how to relate to your thought patterns with more objectivity and equanimity. So, before we get into how to relate to our thoughts, it's vitally important that you be familiar with how to access the stability that arises from turning your attention to the context of your being. If you don't have experience in acknowledging awareness beyond the content of your mind, you will likely get lost or disoriented when we attempt to examine your mental patterns.

Gathering Attention

Over the course of a single day, our attention is pulled into thousands of places. If your mornings are anything like mine, between showering, getting children out the door, and sifting through e-mail, your attention has been pulled in about fifty different directions by 9:00 a.m. When we begin to access the clear mind, we need to first have a place to gather our attention, and the most effective way to do that is through meditation.

The word "meditation" conjures up a lot of different interpretations for people, but for our purposes, I encourage you to think of it as a way to gather your attention and energy. Meditation isn't only an activity, such as being silent and still; it's a way of being. Meditation is an inward journey and contemplative experience. Meditation is rooted in ancient wisdom traditions and not associated with a specific religion or religious tradition. However, nearly every world religion encourages taking time for some sort of silence or inward contemplation as way of accessing clarity. Some traditions call it meditation; others call it repetitive prayer, contemplation, silence, self-reflection, inquiry, or simply quiet time. If your mind conjures up a negative association with the word "meditation," don't fight it; just pick a word that does work for you. Fundamentally, what I'm talking about here has to do with gathering your attention by turning inward.

I've been on my own journey of dropping into presence for years, and I resisted meditation at first. I had to experiment with present-moment awareness in a variety of ways before I began to understand the potency of meditation. Before I started meditating, I directed my mindful attention to what I was doing in the moment, what I was eating, how I was relating, and my thought patterns— all of which led me to deepened levels of clarity and vitality. Then, as happens in life, there came a time in my development where I naturally became curious about meditation and realized my resistance was no longer there, without any concerted effort on my part. I simply stopped resisting my own resistance and naturally became drawn to meditation.

I speak about meditation now because, in my experience, there is nothing that replaces the clarity and awareness that come from meditation. There is a lot of research and discussion across just about every industry about the benefits of meditation, and as I have watched the conversation unfold, I have been simultaneously inspired and concerned. While many companies, sports teams, and public service organizations are experiencing the profound results of meditation, I have also noticed through my work that for some people, meditation has become something they check off their self-improvement to-do list, rather than exploring it as a journey that has the capacity to profoundly change their orientation to life.

The Why of Stillness

While many people meditate to relieve stress, increase performance, and become more centered and focused, meditation offers a deeper possibility. Meditation can be the doorway for you to explore and inquire about the nature of your reality and the possibilities of your existence. Through stillness and silence, you have an opportunity to see that you are not the content of your mind, but rather something far more stable, consistent, nonjudging, and aware. You are pure awareness, with no need to judge, prove, strive, or struggle.

When I started meditating, I struggled with "quieting my mind" and didn't know that letting go of that struggle was an option. I thought struggle was part of the deal with meditation. In fact, that idea of not struggling in meditation (and life) was foreign to me. I was still in a place on my journey where I thought meditation would give me something. I didn't know what it was, but I felt like it should have a "more concrete benefit" than access to peace, stability, or flow. However, from my vantage point now, I see that there isn't any other reason more valuable to me than accessing my authentic nature. Having that stable ground beneath me, after all, allows me to navigate the unpredictable terrain of my external world with more grace and joy.

Since I covered the most fundamental "why" of meditation, let me also share some of the beneficial side effects you may experience as you explore or continue to meditate. I call them side effects because some or all of these are things you may experience through strengthening your attention and deepening your awareness, but the experience is, of course, different for every person.

- **Increased ability to focus:** Because our attention is so fragmented, it has become increasingly difficult to focus or concentrate on one thing at a time. Plenty of research has proven that multitasking is not nearly as effective as focusing on one thing, so, initially at least, meditation is a great way of training your mind to concentrate on one thing at a time.

- **Less reactivity:** Research shows that consistent meditation reduces the size and strength of the limbic system's fight-or-flight response and instead strengthens the neuropathways to the resourceful frontal lobe.[9] As you access the stable ground of your being and become aware of your thoughts and emotions, you will naturally become less reactive. You will begin not to be carried away by thoughts, nor will external events take you off center as easily.

- **Calm of the nervous system:** Many of us operate from a fairly constant adrenalized, fight-or-flight state. As a result, our nervous system is being taxed. Meditation is a way for us to return to our natural, calm state. Granted, you may not experience "calm" the first few times you meditate, because your nervous system also follows a pattern, but through meditation you can give your nervous system a reference point of calm so it, too, can remember its natural state.

- **Access to creativity:** When you meditate, you strengthen your prefrontal cortex and allow your analytical mind to take a break. True creativity does not and cannot come from the analytical mind, so when you meditate, you give your system a chance to rest and open up to other creative possibilities.

- **Giving insight a place to land:** Similar to creativity, insight is not something you can find; it has to find you. Meditation is a way for you to slow down your system, tune into awareness, and allow it to guide you. Your job is to listen and inquire about the information that is presenting itself to you. As with resting into the current of a river, awareness you will tune into has a way of revealing the very next thing for you to examine or explore. You may not always like what awareness reveals, but the insight will show itself in the perfect time.

My client Eric and I had been working together for a few months. At the beginning of our engagement, I had him start with practicing being present in the moment, and then once he got the hang of that, we started to dig into his mental and emotional patterns. Over four months, he had created enough awareness to be familiar with his triggers and reactive responses, to know that his reactivity was to be examined, and not to let his reactions dictate his actions. When I asked him if he was interested in experimenting with meditation, he agreed.

After about a month of experimenting with meditation, Eric reported that he felt a big difference in his energy level and that he felt calmer and more resilient. He told me he had an unexplainable sense that one of the vendors he worked with was engaged in unethical business practices. He couldn't explain the origination of the feeling and had no evidence but told me his feeling wouldn't go away. Eric and I had already explored his complying tendency and his conditioned desire to keep everyone happy, so the idea of confronting this vendor seemed risky to his low mind, yet Eric possessed a clarity within him to explore his gut sense. We talked though the options of how to handle this situation, and he booked a flight to go visit the vendor to explore his hunch. Even though his low mind was nervous, he had access to a clarity that couldn't be rationally explained and that provided him with the stability he needed to walk through his investigation.

It turned out that Eric's hunch was correct and that the vendor had started in on a project without his company's authorization. Eric also uncovered some other egregious behavior, took immediate action to terminate the relationship, and turned the case over to their legal department. Eric was fully aware of his feelings and thoughts (the content of his mind) as he walked through the process. He could feel the fear of losing this relationship, the fear of being wrong, but the content of his experience didn't take him off center. He was in relationship with the content, but not at the mercy of it.

When I saw Eric at our next session, we talked about meditation and how it was related to this situation. He said, "I don't think there was a one-to-one causation between my meditation and finding this situation, but I do think there was a strong correlation." He went on to explain that his meditation practice gave his mind and heart time for things to "land," and that he was pretty sure if he had been going constantly, the way he had been before, he would easily have missed the subtle information that came into his awareness and stayed in his complying pattern.

I want to emphasize Eric's word "subtle" here, because he nailed it on the head. The awareness that is always available to us is very subtle and takes space and quiet to tune into. If we are constantly "on," never giving our mind or body space to let down and relax, there is no time or space for the information to come in. Giving your system a little space to rest into presence not only feels good but also gives you a way to access your clear mind. In Eric's situation, there was a tangible and measurable benefit to his taking the time to gather his attention and energy, and the best "result" that came from Eric's meditation was the profound level of confidence he felt in taking action that registered as risky. A nice side effect of Eric's clarity happened to be that he saved his company more than a quarter of a million dollars. This is a great example of how when we turn inward first, we are able to navigate our external world with more effectiveness, precision and clarity. Not every one of us may uncover financial savings as a result of meditation, but I have witnessed many people be guided by their own awareness in tangible and valuable ways that have changed the trajectory of their careers and lives.

Setting the Stage for Meditation

When starting out, you should know not only your "why" for meditating, but also your "how." When I started meditating, I was under the impression that the "goal" was to quiet my mind. I would sit down and focus on my breath, and within seconds my mind would encounter a thought that I would try to make go away. I heard from multiple teachers to imagine my thought on a cloud, floating away; I tried (earnestly) to do that, and I ended up spending a good deal of time mentally wrestling with the clouds. I came away from the experience frustrated and not energized at all. Then, of course, I didn't want to do it again, and I found every excuse in the book not to put myself through the struggle of meditating again.

Though it is natural and even okay to experience resistance to meditation, struggling with it isn't necessary, nor is it helpful. I'm going to offer you some ways to think about meditation and techniques that you can experiment with, whether you are an experienced meditator or new to it.

Mindset

For me, having the right mindset or attitude about meditation was a vital part of being inspired to come to and rest into meditation. Anytime I felt like I "should" meditate, I got curious about my mind's story. Did I think I didn't have time? Was I under the impression that something else was a higher priority? By putting a little separation between my resistance and my action, I had a space to remember that I actually felt good after meditation. Again, the idea isn't to think or force yourself into meditation; it's to play with these perspectives and see how (or whether) they shift the way you feel about meditation.

- **You are nourishing your spirit:** My conditioned mind used to resist meditation. Of course it did, since its job is to preserve the status quo, and meditation was new and unpredictable and I wasn't "good" at it. So my mind kept making up the story that meditation was another thing to "do" to make myself better, and, frankly, I didn't need another thing on my to-do list. The moment you start feeling the need to do meditation to make yourself better in any way, just stop, because you'll only be reinforcing a false belief. Instead, I invite you to think about meditation as a way of nourishing your spirit. When I first heard Adyashanti offer this perspective in one of his teachings, it was truly an "aha" moment for me. The perspective of nourishing my spirit had a completely different feel than doing meditation as something to make myself better, or another thing I should do. When I'm thinking about making the choice to meditate or not, or whether I have time or not, I remind myself that this is not another to-do on my list, but rather a way to give attention to what is most important to me: my spirit.

- **Have a beginner's mindset:** Particularly if you are fairly new to meditation, having a beginner's mindset will serve you very well. A beginner's mindset is one of assuming you know nothing. The spirit of beginners is that they know they don't know much, and being deeply curious is enough. Think about children learning something new. They don't judge themselves for not knowing how to do something. Their job is to show up and be curious enough to learn. When you show up to meditation with a curiosity to learn and explore, then you are entering into meditation with an open heart and mind, which is exactly what you need to allow awareness to reveal itself.

- **Allow the resistance to be there:** The resistant thoughts and emotions are just part of the deal with meditation, at least for a while. Don't bother trying to fight, justify, or change the content of your experience. Remember, the content of your experience is only a small part of what the whole experience offers. As with a child having a tantrum, there's no need to give the cranky child all of your attention or get sucked into the tantrum. Simply acknowledge the context of your being. As you turn your awareness to the context, you will likely still hear the tantrum in the background, but it doesn't have to dominate your attention. This may be easier said than done at first, but the more you experiment, the more you will learn.

- **Quality over quantity:** I work with a lot of type-A overachievers, and I notice that when I introduce meditation to them, they immediately want to "master" it. Then, when they sit down for twenty or thirty minutes, they become frustrated, for all the reasons I mentioned above. Please, for your sake, value quality over quantity. Two or three minutes of quality attention is more valuable than ten to fifteen minutes of fragmented attention. Start off with small increments of time, but make them consistent. Then, when you are ready (and you'll know when that is), you can experiment with what it's like to meditate for longer periods of time.

- **Meditation is a mirror:** Meditation will reflect back to you what is happening inwardly. That may or may not be something your low mind is interested in, but I suspect the deeper knowing essence in you is very interested in bringing consciousness to that which has been unconscious. There is no rationality or logic to willingly entering into the occasional discomfort of introspection. That's why it's has to come from a deeper longing. The beauty of meditation is that if your inner knowing is leading, awareness will support you in ways you cannot imagine by helping you see what needs your attention and guiding you in how to move forward.

The most important thing about meditation is that you enter into it with a spirit of curiosity, gentleness, nonjudgment, and compassion. Believe it or not, all of those attributes already exist within the context of presence, and meditation will give you the space to access them more easily. There's no better way to remember your natural state than to experience it through meditation.

Technique

The method I'm offering here is for seated meditation, and later I'll offer methods for micromeditation and moving meditation. There are a lot of forms and methods of meditation, and a wide variety of teachers. What I know for sure is that there is not a one-size-fits-all method of meditating, and it's a deeply personal choice. The intention with meditation is for you to access the context of experience—presence itself—so if you already have a practice that helps you access the context of your being, then please keep doing it. Also, if the methods and experiments I offer don't work for you, set an intention to find something that does, and I suspect it will reveal itself to you.

- **Position:** Sitting with a straight and "dignified" spine is ideal for meditation, as it allows the breath to flow freely up and down the spine. If you are unable to sit comfortably, lying on the floor is another good option. Closing your eyes helps bring your attention inward, but if you do not want to close your eyes, turn your gaze to the floor and focus your vision about three to five feet in front of you. The idea is to minimize any extra stimulation, and closed eyes are helpful in doing that. Also, simply place your hands on your lap in a comfortable position, or place your nondominant hand over your dominant hand and allow your hands to rest in your lap. This hand position will help your system explore something other than your standard physical pattern. Rest your tongue just behind your front teeth to allow your jaw to return to its natural, unclenched state.

- **Breath:** Breathing happens naturally, so it is a great anchor to keep coming back to in your meditation experience. Your mind and emotions will forever create content to distract you, and it is easy to get lost in thought. Use the in-and-out rhythm of your breath to gather your attention. Meditation can involve literally hundreds of breath techniques, and I will offer you several later in this chapter, but as you begin to experiment with meditation, just start with a natural breath in and out through the nose. Don't try to force the breath, but rather pay attention to it and where you feel it. Is it in your nose, chest, or belly? Once your system settles down into the stillness and silence, your breath will naturally drop into your belly.

- **Timing:** Experiment with meditating during a time of day that works best for you. Mornings are great because meditation tends to set the tone for the rest of the day, and I notice the days I meditate in the morning often just run more smoothly than mornings I do not. Many of my clients don't have a private space at home, so some sit in their bathroom, or after they drive to work they take ten or so minutes to sit in silence in their car. Given how full our lives are, finding space to meditate can be tricky, but where there's a will, there's a way! If you attempt to meditate at night and find you are simply falling asleep, I encourage you to try a different time of day. By the end of the day, our energy and focus can be quite low, so it's common to fall asleep, but sleep is different than the reflective nature of meditation. However, if I am having a hard time falling asleep, I often use a body scan (pg. 36-37) to relax me enough that I can fall asleep.

- **Length:** Again, the most important thing about meditation is the consistency and quality of your attention, not the quantity of minutes you are in meditation. Although research on the results of meditation is still in its early stages, and there is not yet an agreed-upon "minimum" recommended amount of meditation, we know from other research, in both human behavior and neuroscience, that consistency in action is what eventually changes a pattern or habit. If you are just beginning to experiment with meditation, you may want to start dropping in with just a few aware breaths consistently and work yourself up to two minutes, then four and so on. Just start where you are, and don't allow your mind's commentary to derail you from the experience.

- **Guided meditation:** In a guided meditation, a teacher or facilitator leads you through a meditation in person or via a recording. A lot of my clients ask if they should or should not use guided meditations, or if there is a difference. In my experience, people new to meditation tend to enjoy guided meditation, as it helps them to focus on another person's voice and follow the teacher's prompts. After you have some experience, you will know whether you prefer guided meditation. For me now, there is nothing more replenishing than sitting in pure silence, experiencing the context of my being and all it has to offer.

- **Sensations during meditation:** When I started meditating, I experienced waves of energy moving through my body and images that surprised me. It's common to experience a wide variety of unexpected sensations or visuals during meditation or silent reflection. When this happens, feel free to notice it; there's no need to try to make it stop. But always bring your attention back to your breath so you don't get swept away in the experience. Your entire system (body, mind, and heart) begins to recalibrate to your natural state of calm, and it's just like opening up that junk drawer: some things need to come to the surface so they can get cleared out. You are not "doing" the clearing; your presence is guiding it. By meditating, you create space for awareness to do the clearing. You are always at choice about how you proceed in your experience, and if the sensations become too overwhelming, it's okay to open your eyes and reorient yourself to the present moment.

Meditation is extremely personal and will take time to experiment with what works for you. I have found a lot of joy in trying new techniques, locations, and lengths until I found a way that works for me. Meditation is a sacred time for you, and I encourage you to claim this time for yourself as a way to nourish yourself in the midst of your full life.

Progressive Meditation Experiments

I know we all like to feel competent and successful at just about everything we do, but I invite you to let that thought go when it comes to meditation. There is no fast track with this one; it just plain takes time and attention. However, the great news is that you can access your awareness anytime, including in the middle of your most mundane activities. As you read through the following exercises, keep in mind that every one of them is considered a practice in self-directed neuroplasticity—meaning that with every acknowledgment of awareness, you start creating or strengthening new neuropathways in your brain. That doesn't mean the old neuropathways of your conditioning will go away, but every time you turn toward awareness, silence, and quiet, you "jump the track" and strengthen your new pattern of presence. Read through the following experiments, and start wherever you feel you will be stretched. If this is all new to you, fantastic—start from the beginning. I truly look forward to what is in store for you as you tune into deeper presence.

1. Take a Breather

Because your breath is automatic, it's a powerful way to anchor your awareness back to presence. The good news is that you breathe all day, every day, so you have plenty of opportunity to bring your awareness to it. Your breath is also a great data point for you to see how your body is responding in the moment. When we are stressed, anxious, or tense, our breath gets shallow and fast. Just notice where your breath is in this moment. Is it in your chest, or can you feel it down into your belly? Your natural state of breath is in the belly. Think about when you watch a sleeping baby, whose breath is naturally in their belly; you can see their belly expand and fall with each breath. But for most of us, our daily experience of the breath is shallow in our chest.

You can take a breather anywhere and anytime as way of experimenting with meditation. The first part of taking a breather is simply to notice your breath. After you notice your breath, pay attention to its quality, depth, and speed. Then notice if you can allow it to come down into your belly a bit more. It's important that you not try to force the breath, but rather that you allow your system to let go just a little bit so the breath can drop into your system. Breathe in through your nose and gently out through your mouth. Not only is this practice a powerful way to tune into presence, but the act of taking three conscious breaths is cleansing to the system. You may notice that you feel better after just taking some deeper breaths.

2. Stop and Drop In

The purpose of this experiment is to create several "pauses" in your day so you can drop into presence and remember the context of your being. The moment you wonder, "Am I present?" or, "What am I acknowledging right now?" or, "What am I paying attention to?" you have immediately shifted your consciousness. You can use any moment of your day to stop, drop in, and turn your attention, even for just a moment, to the context of your being. The goal is to see whether you can access the stillness and unchanging nature of the context of your experience, rather than ever-changing content of your mind. Can you shift your awareness out of the content and see what it feels like not to be consumed by your thoughts, even for just a moment? Can you feel the gap and space between your thoughts?

See if you can do this ten to twenty times a day and see what starts shifting with your mind and body. I do this exercise when I'm washing my hands, doing dishes, and taking a shower. I stand there and bring my attention to feeling my feet on the ground, sense what it going on in my body, take a few cleansing breaths, and then, even for a micromoment, rest into the awareness of the context of the moment, remembering that I'm not just a human *doing* but a human *being*.

3. Moving Meditation

Many people ask if running, yard work, yoga, walking, and other exercise "count" as meditation. My answer is, it depends. You can bring the body into movement with awareness and intention, and you can also move the body with relative unconsciousness. For example, I know a lot of runners who use running as a way to practice awareness by really listening to their heartbeat, being mindful of their body's messages, and moving beyond the content of the mind, and they consider running "moving meditation." I also know a lot of runners who push themselves quite hard, don't listen to their body, and are checking yet another accomplishment (another marathon, personal record, and so on) off their list.

Sometimes one of the best things I do, especially when I'm emotionally triggered or lost in the content of my mind (yes, that still happens), is to move my body and bring my attention to the microexperiences within the movement. Although moving meditation is fantastic on many levels, it does not replace the impact of being still. When our bodies are in complete stillness, our nervous system has a chance to relax in a way it cannot when we are moving. Stillness allows our sympathetic nervous system (threat response) to rest and in turn allows our parasympathetic nervous system (rest and digest response) to take over and rest in ways it cannot while moving.

4. Box Breathing

Box breathing is a popular breathing technique used by athletes, military personnel, and mindfulness experts alike. The technique is very simple: breathe in through your nose for four counts, hold for four counts, breathe out through your nose for four counts, hold for four counts. Repeat at least three times or for as long as you desire. Box breathing is an effective way of immediately calming your nervous system and regulates your fear response. I like it as a way of not only calming down the nervous system but also practicing bringing my focus to one thing.

It takes practice to concentrate on one thing, so any of these breathing techniques can strengthen your ability to concentrate. Then, when you have more practice in concentration, you will naturally be able to tune into awareness and explore the greater context of your being beyond the mind.

5. Counting the Outbreath

I first heard about this technique from Adyashanti, who said that when he started meditating, as a way of building his concentration, he would take a breath in through his nose, and on the outbreath he would count "one." Then, on the next outbreath, he would count "two," and so on until he reached ten. He remembers not being able to get to three without getting lost in thought or the content of his experience. When that happened, he would start over at one.

Eventually, he was able to get to ten, and then start over several times in one sitting. He explained that we want to give ourselves *just enough* technique that we can concentrate, but not so much that we lose sight of the experience of dropping into presence. Remember, these "techniques" are just doorways for you to experiment with and practice for gathering your attention; eventually, your system will be able to rest into silence and presence on its own.

6. Anchor Words and Phrases

The use of anchor words, phrases, or sometimes-called mantras is another way for you to focus your attention. When the mind is focused on one thing, like the breath or phrase, it can move away from the fragmented thoughts of the day and into a more focused awareness. The way you use anchor words is very similar to counting breath or focusing on the outbreath, but instead you bring your attention to one word or phrase.

For example, with your eyes closed, inhale through the nose, and on the exhale say a word to yourself, such as "peace" or "stillness." Inhale again, and then, on the next exhale, use the same word or phrase for as long as you'd like. Here are some more examples of single anchor words or phrases that you may enjoy focusing on:

- Silence
- Rest
- Relax
- Presence
- Awareness
- Surrender
- Freedom

Phrases:
- I am here.
- Here and now.
- All is okay.
- Present moment.
- Life is happening.
- Let go.
- I am safe.

The anchor word or phrase can be used to gather attention and focus and can be very helpful as you settle into your meditation. However, if you use anchor words or phrases, be sure to allow yourself to experiment with *not* using the anchor words in the second half or near the end of your meditation. This will allow you to enter into complete silence and to explore where your meditation takes you without guiding or controlling it in any way.

7. Falling into Silence

All of the methods and techniques above are very helpful in strengthening your ability to concentrate, focus your attention, and change the neuropathways in your brain. However, eventually the need for technique or method will fall away and you will simply drop in and explore the vastness of your being.

Eventually you will feel so familiar with dropping in and with the context of your being that even the concept of "context and content" will no longer be relevant to your experience. You will rest into the silence and the experience of just being. I use the language "falling into the silence" because at some point you will spontaneously and completely surrender to the experience of pure silence and presence. There will be absolutely no need for control, no destination or need to understand the mystery of it all. Your experience will be unique and personal and, I suspect, profoundly valuable and sacred. This will all come with intention, time, and commitment to the exploration.

Meditation is not about figuring things out, adding commentary to your mind's narration, or trying to control your experience. In fact it's quite the opposite. It's about the art of nondoing, and nonefforting, which I will describe in the next chapter. Meditation is a space to rest into your awareness, experience the context of your being beyond your conditioned mind, and remember your natural state of presence. I invite you to enter into meditation (or whatever you decide to call it) with a spirit of ease and nonstruggle.

Acknowledging Mind Stories

Once you have experience with accessing a clear mind and the stability of your presence, you will be equipped to examine some of the tactics the conditioned mind uses to keep you on autopilot. There is absolute value in examining the content of your mind, but it's just not the first place you should start. As you know by now, the low mind looks at your current experiences through the lens of past emotional memories and is wired to sort, judge, and quickly make meaning out of your experiences. When we're on autopilot, we aren't even aware that this part of the brain is at play, and the stories it creates can feel awfully compelling.

Two clients attended the same high-stakes meeting and had two completely different experiences. My client Josh told me that it was "obvious" that the leader of the meeting was stressed, reactive, and not at all present. I asked Josh what led him to believe this to be true, and he told me that the leader repeatedly checked his phone, asked the same questions over and over, huffed a lot, and failed to make a tough call on an important decision at the end of the meeting because he was visibly frustrated.

Another of my clients, Chris, told me it was "obvious" that this same leader of the meeting didn't like him. When I asked Chris what led him to believe this to be true, he told me how the leader continuously checked his phone when speaking, asked him the same questions over and over in different ways, and ultimately was not supportive of Chris, because he didn't make the decision to use the go-to-market strategy that both Chris and Josh developed.

It was clear to me that one of my clients took the leader's behavior very personally, while the other did not. We see this playing out all the time in different scenarios where two people experience the same thing and end up having two very different reactions. Let's take a look at what causes us to lose objectivity and start to take things personally.

Even though both Josh and Chris had to present their collaborative go-to-market strategy, Josh was able to participate from a state of presence. He was on solid ground, aware and clear. Josh was not clouded by his own reactivity or need to "look good." He saw the situation for what it was—just another meeting—without making a story about what the outcome meant about him or his worth to the company.

Chris, on the other hand, was clouded by his reactivity, and his low mind interpreted the leader's behaviors as *very* personal. His low mind got hold of same data Josh observed (phone checking, repetitive questions, and so on), and, without conscious thought, Chris's low mind made up a story about what the data meant *about him*. When we are operating on autopilot and not actively exploring our patterns, our low minds can make up a lot of stuff and what it means about us. Our conditioned minds are meaning-making machines, constantly looking for evidence to reinforce our thoughts about any given experience.

When Chris and I started to talk through this experience and story about the leader not liking him, we traced the origin of this particular "story" back to one of the first times Chris met this leader. He told me how the leader wouldn't look Chris in the eye; he didn't smile at him and asked a very pointed question that took Chris by surprise. Chris told me that he just "knew" this guy didn't like him, and it's been like that ever since. Remember, our low mind is always scanning our environment for threat, and, without having to think about it, Chris's low mind labeled this leader as a threat. It had already created a story based on his first experience with this leader and had unconsciously been on the lookout for more data to reinforce the story, which is exactly what our low minds do if left unexamined.

As Chris and I talked through this situation, I asked him if he'd be willing to explore a new idea. "Let's assume (for now) that this leader's behavior had nothing to do with you," I told him. "Let's assume that he doesn't have ill will toward you, and—who knows—maybe even likes you. Either way, let's play with the assumption that his behavior has nothing to do with you. If that were the case, what else could explain his behavior?"

Chris immediately said, "Well, I have no idea, because I'm pretty damn sure this guy hates me." I stayed with him and encouraged him to move beyond his reactivity, until he was able to articulate a different answer. He then said, "Well, I know his division is under a lot of scrutiny right now."

"What else?" I asked.

"I don't think he has very good people skills, either," he said. "In fact, I don't think I've ever seen him smile."

Chris and I continued to explore some additional possibilities, and through our conversation he visibly began to relax. Granted, we were just exploring other "stories," none of which we could confirm with certainty, but it helped Chris to move beyond his reactivity and explore that there might be other reasons for the leader's behavior. Our conversation helped Chris come out of the spell his reactivity had him under. Chris told me that it had never dawned on him that this leader was under so much stress, and depersonalizing the experience actually helped him explore other possibilities about this leader's behavior and how to respond. But Chris couldn't see the situation with clarity because he had been under the spell of his reactive mind.

I explained to Chris that one of the worst things we can do (something that causes much unnecessary suffering and turmoil) is to meet someone's unconscious behavior with our own unconscious behavior. When we aren't present in the situation, we are unable to see our own or other people's reactivity with clarity. This sets us up for a cycle of frustration, anger, and deep misunderstanding. Chris was eventually able to identify that when he first met this leader, he felt dismissed by him, and that triggered his fear of someone (especially someone in a position of authority) not liking him, which was part of his reactive tendency of compliance. I reminded Chris that our work together wasn't about never getting triggered; instead, it was about how quickly he could come to identify his reactive pattern and how he could bring himself back to presence.

Tools for Working with Mind Stories

In *The Four Agreements: A Practical Guide to Personal Freedom*, by Don Miguel Ruiz, one of the agreements is "don't take anything personally." This agreement is simple to understand, though not always easy to follow, especially because our low mind is wired to take darn close to *everything* personally. Remember, this part of our system was designed for survival and uses external factors to define our identity, so of course it takes our life experiences and puts them through its filter of "it's about me."

One of the quickest and most liberating means you can use to elevate your thinking from "everything is about me" to clarity is an examination of your stories by experimenting with these three tools:

1. What If This Wasn't About Me?

When you find yourself stuck in a story or are in a triggered state activated by something external, ask yourself, "What if this wasn't about me?" or, "What else might be going on for this person?" or, "Assuming this isn't about me, what else might explain this situation?"

This tool will help elevate your thinking from your low mind to your high mind, where you have access to a more sophisticated and complex way of thinking. Remember, your low mind is always looking for evidence and patterns to reinforce the identity it has created about who you are in the world. You are not your thoughts or emotions, so the goal in using this tool is to create space between your external situation and your response to it. This will allow you to examine your assumptions and their usefulness and ultimately to stop reinforcing your identity based on your external experience.

2. Externalize the Story

When I heard author Brené Brown speak about her book *Rising Strong*, she talked about the power of externalizing our stories by actually saying, "The story I'm telling myself is . . ." For example, a colleague of mine hadn't responded to an e-mail I sent (about a sensitive topic), and though I really had no reason to believe she would be angry or upset, I felt my mind starting to create a story about her delayed response. So, instead of letting my low mind run amok, I first took a few conscious breaths to bring my attention back to the present moment, and then I called her. I said, "Hi. I'm calling about the e-mail I sent yesterday. The story I'm telling myself is that you are mad about what I wrote."

Then she said, "What e-mail? I didn't get it." I immediately felt relief, because by picking up the phone and sharing what I had going on in my head, I was no longer at the mercy of my busy low mind. Then we were able to talk through what I proposed in my e-mail and handle the situation without causing any further stress.

I loved Brown's articulation of the powerful phrase "the story I'm telling myself is . . . ," because externalizing the story of your low mind immediately lessens some of its power over you, and then you have the ability to start seeing situations with more clarity. In my experience of using this tool, it is extremely powerful in defusing tension and building connection with others. When I shared my mind story with my colleague, she asked, "Why would you think I wouldn't respond to you?" Then it opened up a deeper conversation about being dismissed being one of my triggers, which led to a deeper understanding of a piece of my reactive tendency that I could work with. If I hadn't externalized my story to my colleague, it could have created more internal tension for me and I might have missed out on an opportunity to have a deeper awareness of myself as well.

3. Check Your Accuracy

My client Suzanne told me about some upcoming layoffs at her company, and although she had the list of people she had to let go, she was worried that she was on her boss's list of people who were going to lose their job. She told me that she was "pretty sure" she wasn't going to get laid off, and then gave me all sorts of evidence that supported her belief that her job was secure, yet she kept saying, "I'm probably being silly here, but I'm just worried I'm wrong and am going to lose my job."

Suzanne also told me she was planning to make a big

purchase on a new boat and that if she knew she was going to get laid off, she wouldn't buy it. "If this has a hold on you," I said, "why don't you just ask if you're going to get laid off?" She first just laughed at my suggestion and then told me if she was going to get laid off, her boss wouldn't tell her anyway. We continued to discuss the situation, and I explained to her that her options were to continue to worry over the next couple of weeks, which would drain her energy, or to simply confirm the accuracy of her concern with her boss. If her boss didn't want to share anything, then she was no worse off than she was in this moment. She agreed that there were only upsides to asking, so she mustered up the courage and asked.

She reported back to me that she spontaneously stopped by her manager's office and said, "Hey, I'm thinking about buying a boat this weekend, but I don't want to if I'm going to get laid off. What do you think?" He laughed and said, "Go buy your boat and have a great weekend."

I can't tell you how powerful it is to externalize your stories and then to check their accuracy. My husband and I have used these tools for years, and we have worked through many misunderstandings with more grace as a result. I'm not saying that the stories your mind comes up with will always be wrong; in fact, sometimes when my husband and I externalize our stories, we find that there is an important grain of truth in them that then leads us to powerful and important conversations. Externalizing our stories doesn't mean you don't take responsibility for your part in a dynamic; rather, it's a tool to help you cut through the unnecessary (and often inaccurate) thoughts and emotions wrapped up in a given situation.

As you begin to drop in, it may feel messy, uncontrollable, and even difficult at first, just like when you start to unload that junk drawer, but it's a very important and empowering step in sifting through your conditioning and accessing the solid ground of your being. Then, as a result, I suspect you will feel a deeper level of presence, liberation, and clarity that will evoke a desire to keep dropping into deeper and deeper levels.

CHAPTER 5—Accessing Your Connected Heart

The more you are motivated by love, the more fearless and free your action will be. —Dalai Lama

THE MYSTERY AND CAPACITY of the heart is one of the biggest phenomena of the human experience. It inspires and moves people, yet many people are cut off from giving and receiving love. Our hearts can get bogged down with exhaustion, pain, anger, resentment, and suffering, and we can lose sight of our ability to access the purity of energy of our hearts. In this chapter, we are going to explore what it takes to connect with the heart through the act of listening, first to ourselves, then to others. Then we'll talk about what to do when we connect with our hearts, regardless of the feelings we discover there. Throughout this chapter, we will explore how to be in relationship with uncomfortable emotions and how to connect back to the purity of our connected hearts anytime, anywhere.

Unfortunately, we often see demonstrations of the power of the connected heart after a tragedy. In the aftermath of 9/11 and many devastating disasters since then, we have repeatedly seen people come together in kindness, compassion, and love in deeply moving ways. I believe that the feeling of love—not just romantic love, but deep compassion, kindness and caring for other beings—is a reflection of our natural state of presence.

Love is intrinsic to presence. From a state of presence, you can experience that presence *is* love, and since presence is your natural state, so is the unchanging and unconditional nature of love. In this chapter, we are going to explore how to connect with the heart and our intrinsic compassion. Then we will explore what to do with the information—the good and the bad—when we open our hearts. We will learn how to be in relationship with uncomfortable emotions and how to connect back to the purity of our connected heart anytime and anywhere.

The Transformational Power of Listening

Have you noticed how seldom people really listen to each other? At work, at home, or in our communities, our ability to slow down and truly listen to each other is at an all-time low. The art of listening has fallen by the wayside as the use of technology has increased and our attention has become fragmented.

Deep listening is one of the purest expressions of presence. When we are deeply listening to ourselves or to someone else, we drop into deep awareness, which is why it feels so good to be truly listened to. When someone listens with no judgment or agenda, we are in a field of pure presence that gives insight a place to reveal itself. Have you ever had an experience where someone really listened to you without inserting their opinions or agenda and you spontaneously got more clarity about the situation, or even figured out the solution to your dilemma? This is the power of deep listening. It creates a field of awareness, and simply sitting in that awareness can lead you to the next step or clarity you need to move forward.

When I went through training to become a coach, one of the first things I learned was that in order to fully listen, and not get trapped into thinking that I had to provide the answers, I had to rest into the assumption that each person I interacted with was already whole, capable, and resourceful. This perspective was both profound and liberating for me. The thought of *not* having to provide an answer or anything but a space for people to access their own wisdom was different from anything I'd learned up to that point, yet the truth of this assumption resonated with me. Assuming that people are whole, capable, and resourceful also shifts how you listen. Listening is a powerful doorway to allow clarity to reveal itself. Philosopher and poet Mark Nepo sums up the power of listening beautifully in his book *Seven Thousand Ways to Listen*: "Whatever difficulty you face, there are time-tried ways you can listen your way through. Because listening is the doorway to everything that matters."

The Underpinnings of True Listening

In order to really listen, you must enter into the act of listening with a spirit of openness, spaciousness, nonjudgment, and not being attached to outcome. This is easier said than done, but when done well, the act of listening can transform decision making, negotiation, and the quality of relationships.

When I was halfway through writing this book and on a very tight deadline, the head of my marketing team wanted to revisit the title of this book, *Drop In*. She shared with me her concern that my audience might not understand what I was trying to convey. When she told me that, I felt my stomach sink. I heard my mind reacting and saying, *Are you kidding me? I'm halfway done, and the entire editorial slant is based on the title.* Luckily, I knew that reaction came from my low mind, so I did what I teach others to do: I took a few centering breaths and dropped into curiosity. Rather than defend my title, I said, "Okay, tell me more about your thoughts," and I actually meant it. I wanted to understand where she was coming from and to remain open to the possibility that I might want to change the title. I listened without needing to prove my point, without needing to keep the title or even come away with an answer from this discussion. I kept breathing and asking questions and heard her concerns and ideas. In the course of the conversation, I mentioned that the term "drop in" was used by many wisdom teachers and mindfulness practitioners in describing the experience of turning inward. I then shared with her that in a corporate workshop I attended, led by one of the sports psychologists for the Seattle Seahawks, he used the term "drop in" with us, the participants, and referenced it when he told us a story about teaching the players about meditation. That got her curious, in turn. Now she was asking me to tell her more, and we opened up a conversation in which we were meeting each other on mutual ground. I felt the energy of the conversation shift, and our interaction turned into a creative collaboration from which we both got more clarity and energy about the direction in which we were going with this book.

If there were ever a place where I could have gotten attached, defensive, or stressed, it would have been in this conversation. I cared so deeply about the content of this book, about how it was positioned, and about being a great collaborator and meeting the deadline that I could have easily been distracted by my own interests and defending my point. What would have happened if I didn't really, fully listen with curiosity or if I'd been defensive? Would the conversation have had the same outcome? Would it have strengthened our relationship? Would we both have been as energized about the book? I don't think so.

I haven't always been able to move from being triggered to curiosity so quickly as I did with the head of my marketing team. Like most of us, I spent a good deal of my adulthood not fully listening and mostly trying to get heard. Through my own learning about presence, and in particular about the transformative power of deep listening, I've learned the art of listening and how to stay present while doing so. And through this learning, I've discovered that there are three underpinnings that support the act of listening: the art of nondoing, the art of nonknowing, and the art of nonattachment. Although all of these underpinnings are art forms within themselves and can—and have been—studied for decades before one can master them, read them now, as they relate to the power of listening, both to yourself and to others.

The Art of Nondoing

The art of nondoing is also known as *wu-wei* and refers to a state of being in which our actions are quite effortlessly "going with the flow." In the Taoist tradition, it means to behave in a completely natural, noncontrived way. Nondoing doesn't mean you are just quiet, still, and not taking action; rather, it means that you are not contriving or manufacturing action where it is not needed. In my example above, when I dropped into true curiosity and listened to the points the head of my marketing team was making, I rested into the art of nondoing. I relaxed and allowed the conversation to flow and emerge organically.

Many of us listen with the intent to help, provide, fix, direct, or drive a particular outcome. When we listen with any agenda or need, we are listening from a state of effort, not nondoing. The art of nondoing means that you are first in a state of presence. You are calm and alert, ready to flow with whatever emerges.

I presented the art of nondoing to the top leadership team of one of the world's largest energy companies. I asked each person to find a partner. The exercise that followed involved one person talking about a current challenge they were facing for five straight minutes, without the other person saying anything. You should have seen their faces when I said there was nothing to "do" but rest back and simply listen to their partner! This was a room of all men, no one spoke English as their first language, and, as top leaders of their divisions, they were accustomed to getting stuff done quickly. Needless to say, the idea of resting into nondoing felt very counter to most of their conditioning.

After the exercise, I asked the group, "What was this like for you?" Many of them said it was difficult simply to listen, or even to sit still for five straight minutes. Others said they really enjoyed it but admitted they still had a hard time believing *just* listening was productive or helpful. I then asked the group of people who did the talking to raise their hands if they gained clarity on their situation or even found a solution. Three-quarters of the room raised their hands. This exercise opened up a rich conversation about the power of listening and the counterlogical art of nondoing and ultimately how they could apply this to their everyday interactions. I know it might not make "sense" to the analytical and conditioned mind, but the art of nondoing is an entry point to true listening and allows a space for clarity to reveal itself.

The Art of Nonknowing

The art of nonknowing is about not making judgment about what is happening in the moment. This is incredibly challenging because the low mind is all about judging, sorting, and assessing. There is a well-known Taoist fable that has been recounted in countless books and that you can find online. It's sometimes called "Maybe" or "The Farmer's Luck," and it goes like this:

There was an old farmer who worked his crops for many years. One day, his horse ran away. When his neighbors heard the news, they said, "What bad luck." The farmer said, "Maybe."

The next morning, the horse returned, bringing with it two wild horses. The farmer's neighbors said, "What great luck!" The farmer said, "Maybe."

The next day, the farmer's son tried to ride one of the wild horses and broke his leg when he was thrown from the horse. Again, the neighbors said, "What bad luck." The farmer said, "Maybe."

The day after that, army officials came to draft young men to fight in a war. Seeing that the boy's leg was broken, they passed him by. "What great luck!" exclaimed the neighbors. The farmer said, "Maybe."

The art of nonknowing is deeper than the idea that things simply "happen for a reason," although you can see how each event through this story supports the unfolding of the next event. What I love about this fable is how the farmer responded with equanimity. He consistently demonstrated the art of nonknowing by saying, "Maybe." He didn't get wrapped up in judging one event as any better or worse than the other. Every twist and turn in his week (and it was a busy week!) was simply the next thing that happened. As it relates to listening, the art of nonknowing allows us to weather the highs and lows, the ebbs and flows of experience, and to see through to fruition whatever it is that is going to happen, rather than getting stuck or attached.

The Art of Nonattachment

Most wisdom teachers agree that a major source of human suffering comes from being attached to an outcome or desire. Looking back at the conversation with the head of my marketing team, I can see that the source of my low mind's trigger was being attached to keeping the current book title. Once I let go of that attachment, it made room for other possibilities. When we are not attached to a certain outcome or desire, it means that we're no longer trying to control the situation and instead we are brave enough to allow it to unfold organically. Nonattachment doesn't mean you don't care, or that you become emotionless or stop taking action, but rather that you look for ways to move forward with sincere openness, curiosity, and clarity.

When we get attached to an outcome or desire, it immediately clouds our clarity and judgment. We stop seeing what is *actually* unfolding because we're looking at the situation through the clouded lens of desire. When we are clouded by attachment, we start looking at situations as things to manipulate or control and lose sight of what is actually happening.

When I introduce the idea of nonattachment to my clients, some of them wonder how anything could possibly get done if they weren't driven by attachment. What would move them forward if they didn't become deeply attached to an outcome? It is common to confuse attachment with passion or vision. Although you can still get plenty done by being motivated by attachment, it's not always the most easeful road, and sometimes our attachment can actually derail the natural unfolding of a project or initiative. You can absolutely still have vision and passion for things and make effort toward moving your vision forward, but that is very different from getting attached to an outcome.

In 2014, I was (still am) very passionate about making mindfulness and presence training accessible to children in school. I'd been trying to influence my son's school administrators to pilot a mindfulness program. Leaders at my son's school were conceptually on board, but, no matter what I offered, I could not get a program launched. I offered to pay for it, train the teachers, come into the classrooms, and show statistical results from case studies. I tried every way of influencing I knew, yet, after a year and a half, my son's school still was not piloting a program. I was frustrated, and in talking to my husband about it, I realized how attached I had become to the outcome. I thought I was right. I believed that having a mindfulness program in the schools would serve a higher good and be good for my and other people's kids. But, based on how constricted I felt, I knew I had become attached to the outcome. I knew that I needed to let go of what I thought was "right."

With newfound clarity, I started exploring ways in which I could bring mindfulness to children *outside* school, which allowed me to let go of the stronghold I was feeling about what needed to happen in my son's school. Then one day a few months later, I was picking up my boys from school. We were almost to the car when my youngest, Logan, said, "I forgot my homework. Can we go and see if my teacher is still there?"

Feeling annoyed, I agreed, and we turned back. When we stopped by the classroom, his teacher was packing up and just about to leave. One thing led to another, and we ended up having a conversation about my first book, how she was doing some breath training in the classroom, and how she needed more tools to help the kids focus. After a rich discussion about her classroom and my vision, she suggested, "Why don't we bring you in to talk to the kids about mindfulness and try a little pilot in my class?" Needless to say, I was thrilled, and at the time of this writing, the pilot is well under way and the kids and teacher are feeling a positive impact from giving a little time each day to turning inward in silence.

In this situation, once I let go of attachment to a specific outcome, there was a sense of flow, and all the little synchronicities and kismets that accompany being open and nonattached had room to move and guide me. Being nonattached doesn't mean you can't have a preference or desire, but there's a subtle energy behind your actions, and it's important to realize how they impact your interactions with others, and to clarify the difference between vision and attachment.

As you experiment with nonattachment, specifically as it relates to listening to yourself and others, be sure to keep checking yourself to see if you have become attached to a certain outcome. The moment you have decided a certain thing is what *should* or *needs* to happen, you have already convoluted the natural evolution of the conversation and taken a few steps closer to being attached.

Deep Listening

As I suspect you already know, there are different levels of listening. There is surface listening and listening with your whole being. The first level of listening is cosmetic listening. Cosmetic listening— listening at the surface—is being aware that others are talking, or noticing sounds, without particularly paying attention. Cosmetic listening is the lightest-touch listening we can do. Next, there is conversational listening, which is when you are *sort of* listening, but not fully. I'm guilty of conversational listening when I'm cooking dinner and my son wants to tell me all about yet another new character he unlocked in his video game. Or maybe you have been on a conference call but put yourself on mute and continued to work. Conversational listening is when we want people to think we're listening, but we're not fully present. This type of listening is usually an indicator either that we don't care too deeply about the topic being discussed or that it's not a high priority.

Active listening is when you are fully engaged in the conversation and are likely paying full attention. Many people have been trained to think that active listening is demonstrated through

LEVELS OF LISTENING

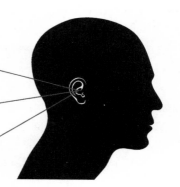

| Cosmetic Listening |
| Conversational Listening |
| Active Listening |
| Deep Listening |

"parroting" back what the speaker said, or asking for clarification. Active listening is characterized by paying a lot of attention to the speaker's words and spending energy to make sure you understand the speaker's point of view. And while active listening may seem to be a high level of listening, there is yet another level: deep listening.

Deep listening is when you listen with your whole being—your body, mind, heart, and gut. Deep listening requires your undivided attention and awareness. You cannot listen deeply if your mind is on something else, or if your attention is fragmented by other distractions, like technology. I suspect you are aware that it is awfully hard to have a deep conversation if your phone or watch is constantly buzzing. I have been known to ask people I'm in conversation with to put their phones or messaging on "do not disturb," just so we have a fighting chance to meet each other with our full presence and attention.

Listening to Yourself

The practice of deep listening to ourselves and to others is primarily the same. However, when I teach people about listening with their whole being, I always start them off with practicing listening to themselves first, because if you can't deeply listen to yourself, you are not going to be able to deeply listen to anyone else.

The act of deep listening is first and foremost about shifting your awareness to the context of your being and acknowledging the spaciousness of presence itself. The interlude and Chapter 4 go into detail on how to do this. For any deep listening to occur, you need to first connect with the stable and aware nature of presence itself. Once you have oriented to presence, the rest of the listening is just that: listening and being curious about what reveals itself.

In the fall of 2014, I was working on a major project. The deadlines were tight, and there was very little wiggle room in the project plan. I woke up one morning with what felt like a cold. I was tired and my nose was stuffy, and the last thing I wanted to do was sit down and force myself through work. Yet part of me knew I needed to get a lot done that day. When I felt the tension between what needed to get done and how I felt, the first thing I did was meditate and create a space to listen to what my body, mind, and heart wanted to tell me. When I sat down and closed my eyes, I tuned into my body's sensations. I could feel how tired I was, how foggy my head was, and how achy I was. I knew I wasn't feeling great, but when I really listened to my body, I was surprised by how not well I felt. Then I acknowledged my relatively loud thoughts about timelines and how I didn't have time to be sick. Again, feeling the tension between my conditioned mind and body intelligence, I reflected on the tenet that awareness knows what it's doing, so I asked myself bravely, "What do you need?"

I immediately heard, "Rest." When I considered taking the day to rest, I experienced a wave of panic, spontaneously followed by a lot of tears. Just the thought of giving my system what I needed in light of a major deadline freaked me out, opening an emotional well. I didn't consciously know how much my mind had been attached to the successful completion of the project, how hard I had been pushing myself, and how hungry I was for reprieve. By deeply listening to all aspects of my being—my body, mind, and heart—I uncovered important information about my experience that needed exploring.

As a result of my Bell's palsy experience, I am more prone to listen to my body in ways I wasn't before. I now know that pushing myself through deadlines and stress is a behavior that can result in sickness. So, despite my fear and my tears, I decided to let myself rest. My mind grappled with how I could make up the lost time, but I didn't let my mind run the show. I honored my deeper knowing that I needed to rest. I stopped struggling and turned off my computer. I slept, read, and took a break from my electronics. I called a friend and asked her just to listen to me. I was "all in" on resting; even though my mind wanted to push me back to work, I just allowed those thoughts to be there. Those thoughts were a part of my awareness, but not the part that dominated the day.

The next day, I woke up feeling better, and when I sat down to work on the project, there was more of a flow and ease to my work than there had been the day before. In fact, I ended up inspired by something I had read during my downtime, and it shifted the direction of the project, which I then completed ahead of my deadline.

When you listen to yourself deeply, awareness will reveal what insight is needed. The question becomes: Are you willing to listen to your knowing? When I created space to listen to myself, I tuned into the reality of my physical body and my system knew exactly what was needed. I had the courage to give myself what I needed with the knowing (through experience) that the most "productive" thing I could do was give myself a much-needed break.

Deeply listening to ourselves is about being aware of the insight that is revealing itself. In my example, the "answer" was relatively simple. But if the knowing you receive is more complicated or seems like something that will need some planning or thought, like needing to make a major lifestyle change or job change, then honor the knowing of that, too. Just because you become aware of insight doesn't mean you need to jump into a rash decision or move. Let your knowing sit in your consciousness, and let it evolve, move, or adjust. The single best thing you can do to shift your experience of life is to turn your attention to awareness.

Experiments in Deep Listening to Self

Listen for Silence

Everything exists within the context of silence, and if you listen deeply, you will hear and sense silence. It may be for only a moment—between words, between notes, between the honks of a car—but silence is present in every situation. Listening for silence is an engaging way to strengthen your focus, attention, and ability to listen. So the next time you are stuck in a waiting room, a grocery line, or even a meeting, see if you can turn your attention to the context of preexisting silence. Another client shared with me that she learned to back herself into listening for silence: she listened for the loudest noise in the room, then listened for the second-loudest noise, and so on, until she could hear the silence in between the noise.

Listen for Insight

Think about a challenge you are currently facing or a place in your life where you desire more clarity. Then start gathering your attention and turn it to the stable ground of presence. After you feel grounded and centered, think about the challenge you are facing and ask yourself, "What's my deepest knowing right now?" or, "What do I need right now?" You may even ask yourself, "What do I know that I wish I didn't know?" The point of this exercise is to create a space where you intentionally listen to your deepest knowing about whatever situation you are in.

Again, you may not like the answer, know what to do with the answer, or even get a clear "answer." Regardless, the practice is about continuing to be intentional about the knowing revealing itself. If you notice that you are starting to work too hard for an answer or insight or becoming attached to finding an answer, just back off from the effort and *rest* into the context of awareness. The next thing you need to know will reveal itself in the right time. Sometimes the power of the experience is about sitting with discomfort of the nonknowing. Your life is always flowing, and the nonknowing will pass, and you may suddenly find yourself with an unexplainable clarity that came from "out of the blue."

Deeply Listening to Others

The art of deeply listening to others is a rich enough topic to warrant its own book. When listening to others, we're not only aware of our own reactions, needs, and demands but also aware of the reactions, needs, and demands of the person we're sitting with. This is why it is so important for you to regularly access the solid ground of presence, so you don't get swept away by your experience or the experience of the person you are listening to.

Assuming you are grounded and present, the act of deep listening can be one of the most generous, loving, and healing things one person can offer another. When we listen from awareness without judgment, without a need to fix, and without being attached to an outcome, then deep listening becomes joyful, easy, and even energizing. This is what makes working with individual clients so enjoyable for me. I can deeply listen to them without needing them to "get" whatever we're working through. The act of me listening allows my clients to become aware of their own insights without major effort on my end. I offer guidance when it's needed, but the foundation of my work is to create a space where others can be listened to deeply without anyone's placing upon them judgment or demands that they do anything differently. It's from this space that everyone can access the intelligence beyond their analytical mind.

Listening deeply to others isn't too different from listening deeply to yourself. The foundation for any listening is to access the stability of presence, then to tune into the overall experience. When I listen to clients, I'm simultaneously listening to their words and noticing my body sensations, thoughts, and feelings as they arise. It's all data to eventually sort through, but as the information first arrives, the only thing I charge myself with is paying attention to the whole experience. When I meet with clients, I have no idea where a conversation might go. People come in with challenges or things they would like to talk through, but very rarely is the conversation linear. Sometimes my clients know where to go, sometimes not. Sometimes one phrase or body sensation is what guides us. Following the breadcrumbs of our collective awareness, the experience turns into a collaborative mystery for us both.

One time in session, my client Debbie was telling me all about a challenge she was facing with finding time on her calendar for herself, because of a project she was working on for her manager. After listening for about ten minutes, I kept getting a very specific visual of her on a white chariot, whipping two white horses. The image was so detailed that I could not ignore it. I had no idea why this visual was coming up or if it had any meaning, but I shared it with her. She immediately stopped talking and asked why I'd used that metaphor. I told her I had no idea, that it had just popped into my mind. "I'm kind of freaked out right now, because when I was growing up, my father always told me that I am the victor of my life and only I can drive my own chariot," she told me.

If I had been listening to Debbie with the intent to help fix, provide, or shift the conversation, we both would have missed out on an important piece of information that revealed itself. I didn't put any effort into manufacturing a metaphor for her, and if I had, I'm confident it wouldn't have been as meaningful for her as the chariot metaphor. Obviously, I did more than just listening here. I participated in the conversation and offered Debbie information that was coming up for me. I also allowed her to talk without interruption. Then, once Debbie had spoken and felt complete with what she had to say, I offered the data that had presented themselves to me.

Experiments When Listening to Others

Uninterrupted Listening

When was the last time you deeply listened to someone else for five or ten straight minutes? I mean *really* listened? I have seen this experiment of uninterrupted listening save marriages, business deals, and relationships with children. The premise of this experiment is to deeply listen, from a place of presence and not needing to fix, prove, strive, or any other efforting on your part. For just a few minutes, you are offering someone of importance true presence without reaction or words from you.

The way you do it is very simple. First, you let the other person know that you are going to fully listen to them without interruption for at least five minutes (but maybe gradually move to ten minutes or more). Then listen to them with your whole being—body, heart, and mind. Pay attention to their words and, more important, to what is under the words. What energy are you sensing? What do you sense they are not overtly saying? For this short time, listen with an open heart and compassion for them as a human being and see how this shifts your relationship or outcome.

Share What Is There

When listening to others deeply, your job always is to listen first from presence, *then* to offer any insight that may have presented itself to you. I call this practice "sharing what is there." This could look like your offering to share your body sensation when the speaker said something specific, such as, "When you said you felt like you had no choice, my stomach immediately tightened" or, "When you started talking about that person, I felt my head get achy." You could also share any emotion or thought that may have popped up for you, such as, "When you spoke about Joe, my first thought was, 'What is it about Joe that has so much power over your mood?'" or, "When you talked about needing to talk to Sue, I started feeling really emotional." Offering this information or data has a very different energy than fixing, judging, or demanding. It's the most powerful way of being in dialogue with the other person without projecting your needs or wants onto them.

Of course, the conversation will continue to emerge after you share your insights, and always keep watching your need to be understood or get your point across. Once you give your full attention to someone, they often spontaneously offer it back. If they don't, you can say something like, "I'm practicing listening more deeply, and I'm wondering how that was for you. Would you be interested in trying it while I talk?" Making a nonattached request is perfectly reasonable, and it is your job to be fully prepared for the other person to either say no or not be able to offer you the same level of presence. I know how disappointing or frustrating it can be not to be fully listened to, and that same disappointment will point you to another level of awareness that may need examining. For example, if you are in a relationship where the two of you cannot give each other the same level of intent to listen (notice I did not say "perfection," but rather "intent"), then that may be a pattern you want to explore.

Turning Toward Emotion

I suspect you know how robust and intense your heartfelt experiences can be. They can offer the deepest love and be the home of some of the greatest fear and pain you can imagine. Throughout this book, I have pointed you inward and offered ways to acknowledge your natural state of presence. Through my experience with my clients, I know that even though turning inward makes sense and people know how to do it, they still feel resistant to it. One of the reasons we are resistant to turning inward is because of the emotions that can get stirred up when we start to examine our inner world.

In one session where I was teaching about presence, I took a group of corporate leaders through one minute of silent breathing. After it was over, I asked the group about their experience. After several people said things like, "It was nice" or, "I felt calm," someone else said, "I don't like it in there—it's scary and dark." I honored her experience and said that we all have different experiences when we turn inward. We are wired to avoid discomfort, so it can almost sound crazy to suggest turning directly toward your emotions so that you can actually feel them. Yet, in my experience, there is no other way through stuck or stored emotion than to let it move through you and feel it. Therefore, I suggest turning toward emotions in order to be free from any grip they have on you.

The moment you turn toward an emotion, it loses some of its power. Ultimately, turning toward emotion alters your relationship with the emotional pattern. Musician Jim Morrison summed it up nicely when he said, "Expose yourself to your deepest fear; after that, fear has no power, and the fear shrinks and vanishes. You are free." There's a strong liberation that comes from moving through unexpressed emotion. It's a process that takes courage for sure, but it's also so worth it.

Emotional Maturity

When you decide to engage with and explore emotional patterns, you start taking responsibility for your emotional life. When you take responsibility for your emotional life, you begin to liberate yourself from being a victim of your emotional patterns. I heard wisdom teacher Adyashanti say, in one of his teachings from his course "The Way of Liberating Insight," that when you take responsibility for your emotional experience, "you become your own resource for emotional freedom," and this act of taking responsibility is emotional maturity.

Emotional maturity comes from deciding that you are no longer willing to be victim to your emotions. That's not to say you won't feel uncomfortable or painful emotions, but instead of letting the emotion chase you and control your experience, you stop running and turn directly toward the emotion with a sense of empowerment.

My first experience of consciously turning toward emotion happened in my midtwenties. I was having recurring nightmares in which the same "monster" was always chasing me, and it frightened me to the core. I couldn't run or move or scream. I felt repeatedly victimized and came to dread falling asleep. My coach at the time introduced me to the concept of lucid dreaming, as well as to the teachings of psychotherapist Carl Jung. The idea behind lucid dreaming is that you can alter the direction and outcome of your dream with your consciousness while in a dream state. I was blown away by the idea that I potentially had some control over my horrible nightmares. The following night, the nightmare happened again. The monster was in my apartment. I'll never forget how vivid the image was and how very scared I was. But this time, I felt a wave of anger come over me. I was dreaming, but I was conscious. I turned around and looked at the monster and asked it, "What do you want from me?"

It said, "Pizza."

I thought, "Are you kidding me? Seriously? *Pizza?*"

You know how dreams go—they don't always make a ton of logical sense—but the feeling I got from my interaction with this monster was meaningful to me. It was the first time I felt on a visceral level that I had a choice about my emotional experience. I didn't have to be afraid, and my fear of the monster was far worse than actually turning toward it. And when I discovered what it wanted, it was almost amusing that this was the monster that had been terrorizing me. Granted, in my dream I had to muster a lot of courage to turn around and face my fear, but ever since then I have had a sense of empowerment around turning toward scary emotions. When it comes to feeling emotion, my motto is "shovel while the piles are small." What I mean by this is simple: don't wait until the emotion has a huge hold on you. Feel it as soon and as deeply as you can so it doesn't grow. By taking responsibility of your emotional experience, you are freeing yourself and others from the tyranny of fear and pain.

Emotional maturity consists of having the intention to take responsibility for your emotional experience and a willingness to allow awareness to guide you through the emotional experience. That means you have to be willing to let the emotion run through your system with a level of surrender in order to be free from it.

Dropping into Emotion

In this next section, I'm going to guide you through how to drop into emotion and metabolize it so you can ultimately be liberated from it. As you read, consider issues or emotions that are mildly irritating or painful. Don't start with the biggest, most painful memory you have.

Most of us aren't used to voicing, expressing, or allowing emotion to move through us in ways that are effective and mature, so you might have a bad picture in your mind when I say "express, feel, or metabolize emotion." But emotion is simply energy in motion; it's designed to move and clear out of your system with relative ease. I don't mean to imply that the process of metabolizing emotions is easy, but you can prevent them from getting stuck, and with practice can move them through and out of your system with a certain grace.

Feeling and expressing emotion is similar to having a gas bubble. I know, it's not an elegant metaphor, but it works. Think about how, when you have a gas bubble, you can feel it brew in your belly. Depending on the size of the bubble, it may be uncomfortable and even downright painful as it makes its way through your system. You might think about what you ate or drank that caused the pain, or sometimes the gas appears without a good cause. Either way, you are acutely aware that your system is in pain, but you also know it will eventually pass. Then, when your system is ready, the gas bubble releases. The gas bubble was in motion, working its way out of your system without a ton of effort on your part, and the same is true of emotions. When you acknowledge the awareness of the emotion, awareness itself helps the emotion move through your system to the surface, and then it clears.

Have you ever had the experience of feeling better after a good cry? A good cry is your body's way of clearing emotion. When you cry, you are metabolizing emotion so it is no longer in your body. Your tears even contain small amounts of toxins (as well as antibacterial agents), so the act of crying literally detoxes your system. Many of us have been conditioned to believe that crying or other healthy forms of emotional expression are not "good." We've all heard the messaging that crying is weak. Our parents tell us, "Don't cry," yet keeping emotions stuck and stored in the system is hurting us more than helping us. Just look at the escalation of violence and depression as evidence. Both are expressions of repressed emotion.

If feeling and expressing emotion in productive ways feels new to you, then please have compassion for where you are. If the experience of dropping into your emotions overwhelms you, know that your breath and awareness of the stable ground of your being are your best anchors into presence. Be sure to be honest with yourself about the need for support. That may be in the form of a coach, counselor, or therapist, and in these initial phases of dropping into the depth of emotion, it can be very helpful to have someone else guiding and supporting you through the process.

The Journey of Dropping into Emotion

The first thing we need to do before we take this journey of dropping into emotion is to make sure you connect with the stable ground of your being. Remember, emotions are the content of your experience, and not the only thing available to you. Before we dive into exploring emotion, close your eyes and, even for a moment, turn your awareness to the context of your being, remembering that *you* are not your emotions, thoughts, or sensations. Your stable ground of your being and your breath is the anchor to reality and safety that you need to remember as you engage with your emotion.

Step In

Think about a situation that you are experiencing that brings up emotion for you. It may be a situation that frustrates you or makes you sad or angry, or even just a little blah. This may feel counter-logical, but I'm asking you to actively poke a tender area in your heart so we can start relating to it with awareness. If you are having a hard time picturing a situation, imagine something you are scared of or don't want. For example, when I took Josh, one of my clients, through this exercise, he told me about a time when he yelled at his son during a baseball game. He knew it was the wrong thing to do, but he was mad about how "flaky" his son was on the baseball field during this game.

You may not need to pick a situation because the situation has already picked you. Go with the first situation that comes up for you, even if it doesn't make a ton of sense.

Rest into the Emotion

Once you have identified the situation, picture yourself in the situation as clearly as you can. Don't just think about the situation, but rather see if you can evoke the emotion that you are feeling or felt in this situation. When Josh closed his eyes, he could remember the visceral feeling of sitting in the stands, watching his son play baseball, and how he kept getting more and more frustrated and angry. When you recall the situation, turn your awareness to the experience and feel how it feels in your body, where there is tightness, heat, constriction, and so on.

By turning your attention to the sensation of the emotion in your body and continuing to focus on the breath, you might not be as tempted to follow your mind's thoughts about this experience. Your thoughts are just more content, and more content is fine but just not where you want to focus right now.

What's Even Deeper?

By feeling the initial emotion, you might notice that your awareness reveals an even deeper emotion that is just beneath the surface. This first emotion is called the primary emotion, and these emotions often reveal themselves in the form of defensiveness, anger, frustration, irritation, resentment, or just feeling blue. If the first emotion you are feeling falls into one of these categories, know that something even richer, called the secondary emotion, is likely waiting to be explored. Secondary emotions usually boil down to fear or sadness/grief.

Give Voice to the Emotion

This part of processing emotion is critically important. It's crucial to have a way for the emotional experience to get out of your body. It's been stuck in there, and that energy needs a place to go. Having someone listen to you, journaling about your experience, or even saying it out loud to the air are all effective ways to get the emotion out of your system.

Dr. Dan Siegel, professor of clinical psychiatry at UCLA School of Medicine, refers to the power of giving voice to the emotion as "name it, to tame it"—meaning, by naming the emotional experience, you allow both hemispheres of the brain to work together to process and make sense of the experience.

Let It Flow

As you continue to turn awareness to the emotion and give voice to it, more waves of emotion may come up. Anyone who has processed grief knows that the pain and emotion come in waves. Once the initial opening occurs, you don't know when the next wave will come, how long it will last, or how intense it will be. This is the part of the process where surrendering to it is your best option.

Trying to stop the flow of the moving energy of the emotion might be harder on your system and psyche than just letting it flow. You've come this far; just keep being with the experience, and allow the emotional pattern to flow and ultimately unravel itself.

Acknowledge Yourself

After the initial waves of emotion have passed, you might feel tired, vulnerable, or disoriented. Those feelings are normal and just come with the territory of processing emotion. It's important, though, that you acknowledge the courage it took for you to step into the unknown territory of your emotion. You were brave enough not to deny or suppress your emotions and instead turned inward to process your emotional life with responsibility.

Please don't step over acknowledging yourself for your courage. I have deep respect for anyone who owns their emotions. Be compassionate with yourself right now. You may not be at your "best" and may be feeling like you went through something major, because you did. It usually takes about twenty-four to forty-eight hours for the residual energy and toxins to release from your body, so, during the initial couple of days, try to be more understanding and gentle with yourself than you might normally be. Be mindful of creating some refuge for yourself in the initial hours or days after the emotional release. It's important to honor what your system is processing. A nice way to help your system process the chemical release you just went through is to drink more water than usual and/or soak in a hot Epsom-salt bath, as salt water is very detoxifying.

The ride of our emotions can feel scary sometimes, but with the right support, orientation, and tools, you can responsibly and effectively navigate the rough waters of your emotions so you can access the power of your heart more easily.

Tools for Connecting to Heart

Sometimes connecting to the power of our heart is all we need to quickly shift our mood and our experience of the world. When I'm feeling down or frustrated or feel as if I have lost perspective, I come back to these tools to help me shift my orientation to life.

Gratitude

The act of gratitude has been proven to reduce blood pressure, improve stress-related illnesses, and alleviate symptoms of depression. Gratitude can come in a variety of forms, such as telling people how you feel, keeping a gratitude journal, or even silently reflecting on things you are grateful for in your life. Adding regular gratitude to your day is a very efficient and potent way for you not only to connect with your heart but also to send that heart energy out into the world.

Start looking for things that you have, rather than don't have. Notice all the ways in which people support you or your lifestyle, and who impacts your life in positive ways. Pay attention to your surroundings—both the physical and nonphysical items—that add to the ease of your life. Even try giving thanks for situations or people that appear to be causing you trouble. You may be surprised at how quickly accessing your heart shifts your perspective.

Assuming Decent Intent

Notice how your heart feels when you assume someone has a bad intent. Maybe you have experienced this when someone cut you off on the road or you felt the impact of a rude grocery clerk or someone at work failed to recognize your contribution. Now notice what it feels like when you assume that person had a decent intent or at a minimum was clueless about the impact they were having on you.

You can radically shift your experience in the world when you experiment with the idea that people are trying to do their best and aren't purposely trying to hurt or offend you. You can take this idea one step further by experimenting with noticing that when people are having a rough day and acting out, they are in pain. When you realize we are all walking around in some level of pain, your heart may naturally express more compassion and kindness toward others, even if they can't give it to you.

Goodwill Meditation

This practice is often called *metta* meditation or loving kindness, and the idea behind this concept is that you spend some time in a quiet, reflective state, actively putting goodwill out into the world. This practice helps you quickly access the natural state of compassion and kindness and, through personal experience, opens your heart in profound ways.

In this meditation, you first center yourself for a few breaths and then wish yourself love, peace, happiness, good health, or whatever kind of well wishes you would like to receive. You can phrase it like, "May I be happy. May I be at peace. May I be kind to myself." Then send well wishes to people closest to you, such as your family, coworkers, or friends. It might sound like, "May Lisa be happy. May my friends be at peace. May my family feel supported."

Then move on to people you consider acquaintances, but not as close to you as your family and friends. These might be coworkers or people you know through your community. Notice if your body sensations shift at all when you start thinking about these people. Simply breathe and send them well wishes. Then move on to strangers and send them the same wishes of peace, happiness, health, and so on.

Then think about a person or people with whom you do not

get along or with whom you are at odds right now. This may feel challenging at first, but, staying connected to your open heart, send them all the positive wishes you have sent everyone else.

I like to end my metta meditations by sending all beings well wishes, by saying:

May all beings be happy.
May all beings be at peace.
May all beings be free.

CHAPTER 6—Accessing Your Courageous Gut

Enlightenment is not for the faint of heart. —Unknown

IF YOU HAVE MADE IT THIS far in the book, consider yourself courageous! Seriously, it takes courage to drop into the unknown world of your conditioned mental and emotional patterns and to entertain the thought of shifting your relationship with those patterns. In addition to courage, we need time and space to reflect, and the demands of our daily lives don't make the job any easier. Our packed schedules at work and home, our constant connectedness to technology, and our tendency to look outside ourselves for purpose, value, and direction are major forces that we have to confront in order to access presence and clarity.

The courage to drop in and examine your thoughts, feelings, and actions can be done only if you are serious about transforming your experience of life. True transformation and awakening cannot be achieved overnight or with any magic pill. It takes a commitment to clarity and a willingness to create the space needed to transform.

Then, with awareness guiding you, you will be presented with the next place in your life to bravely examine and potentially make new choices to support your new level of clarity.

Incremental Courage

Early in my own journey, I would never have considered myself courageous. Initially, my journey was not fueled by a deep desire for awakening or enlightenment. I hadn't set out to "find myself" or to become a teacher. In fact, my journey was fueled by a desire to feel some relief. I wanted relief from my pain, stress, low energy, and sense of imbalance in my life. I realize now that there were some major fork-in-the-road moments that called for courageous action, but the bulk of my courage to keep walking this path came forth through a series of microdecisions that profoundly altered my experience of life.

When any of my teachers spoke about the commitment or courage it takes to be on the path of presence, I felt quite nervous and unsure that I had what it takes to be "successful" at this whole thing. Although I would never now reference the process of shifting consciousness as something a person becomes successful at, back then, it felt like an all-or-nothing deal. My mind panicked at the thought of being "all in" and fully committed. Immediately, my low mind conjured up thoughts of losing the comfort of my home, family, and worldly possessions.

At the time, I knew enough to know what it felt like when my low mind was scared, and I kept moving forward, despite my fear that I wasn't truly committed. All I knew was to take one decision at a time. I learned about what I call incremental courage in the summer of 2000, when I participated in a three-day, sixty-mile walk to support breast cancer research. I had never done anything to push my body like this, but I was curious to see what I could do when challenged. I diligently trained for months and felt as prepared as I could have been for the three days ahead of me.

As the first day approached, weather forecasters were calling for it to be one of the hottest days on record in the Seattle area. After the opening ceremony, we began our twenty-two-mile trek at 9:00 a.m., and it was already eighty degrees outside. None of us was prepared for what we were about to experience, since the average high for summer days there was about seventy-five degrees. By noon, I was experiencing the fallout from not having trained to walk in the heat and was already forming blisters on my swollen, hot feet.

The coordinators of the walk offered pit stops every two miles where we could refuel, rest, and have the option of taking a shuttle to the end-of-the-day campsite. By 3:00 p.m., it was 101 degrees and we were only sixteen miles into the day's walk. People were passing out from heat exhaustion, and my calves had started to blister from the heat radiating off the asphalt. I had serious concerns about my ability to complete the walk, and at every pit stop my walking partner and I checked in to see if either of us wanted to take the shuttle. At every pit stop, I really thought about getting in an air-conditioned bus and fantasized about being finished for the day, but I told my partner, "I'm going to walk to the next pit stop and see how I feel." This became my commitment strategy. I gave myself a true option of choosing to reinvest in the commitment or opt out every two miles.

What I noticed throughout the first couple of days of the walk was that my courage and commitment built on themselves. The more I chose to walk, the more I wanted to walk, even if it was difficult. But the moment I turned my attention to the future and thought about the dozens of miles ahead of me, or started to think about how I could possibly finish, I became overwhelmed and scared. The only thing that kept me in the walk was taking every two miles at a time. By the morning of the third day, I could barely walk because of the blisters I had on nearly every toe. However, I had made it so far, and I really didn't want to stop, so I ended up cutting the toe box out of both of my shoes, and that gave me just enough relief to finish.

When my clients start seeing their lives with more clarity, it's natural for them to become scared or overwhelmed by seeing the changes they might need to make on the road ahead of them. What I found for my clients and myself is that having true courage and commitment comes down to the very next microdecision in front of you. It comes down to the day-to-day, moment-by-moment decisions of choosing sanity and clarity over conditioned patterns.

As you engage in turning inward and make one courageous move to align with awareness, it will naturally propel you to the next choice. Your courage will incrementally build on itself, and if you arrive at a major fork-in-the-road decision about how you live your life, you will be standing there with a track record of courage and you will be able to drop into the clarity of awareness and make the right move for you at the time. Keep in mind that there is no "right" way of being on the path of presence; you simply take the next steps ahead of you and commit to presence. You may stumble, get blisters, or even decide to take an air-conditioned bus to get some relief. No matter what you choose, presence will continue to be available to you, and the more you acknowledge the stable ground of your being, the more courage you will access.

Claiming Space

It takes space and time to drop into presence and transform your relationship to life. Dropping in requires some stillness, rest, reflection, and quiet, and you cannot multitask your way through this one. When I work with my clients, needing space is one of the scariest places they confront, because so many of us are addicted to the level of freneticism of our current life, so it takes courage to go against our conditioning. My clients may not like how busy they are, but on some level they have become accustomed to this extreme level of busyness that's expected of us and that we impose upon ourselves.

I have worked with enough extremely busy professionals to know that there has got to be a deep internal desire to shift their relationship with time and space on their calendars. I cannot, nor will I attempt to, convince anyone to examine their relationship with activity if they do not want to. I have tried, and it doesn't work. Attempting to convince someone who doesn't really want to shift to do so is like trying to talk to an addict who hasn't hit rock bottom yet. The internal desire to change has to exist and to evoke new decisions and actions.

Choosing Space

When I work with clients, I ask them to reflect on their schedule, both at work and outside work. I ask them to reflect on the "why" behind their commitments and how the commitments impact their energy. My clients are often blown away by how much they don't think or feel into their commitments. On some level, they have been on autopilot about their recurring meetings, lack of breaks, children's sporting events, family gatherings, and other commitments. It's common for my clients to be in constant reactivity when it comes to their calendar, and to feel as if they are the mercy of their calendar, rather than the other way around.

One of my clients referred me to his colleague as a result of the progress he'd made in working with me. When his colleague reached out to make an appointment, our busy schedules resulted in the first available appointment being six weeks out. Two days before our meeting, Steve's assistant reached out to say that he needed to reschedule our meeting. The rescheduled meeting was scheduled for four more weeks out. Then the same thing happened again, a last-minute reschedule. By the time we finally met, nearly three months after our initial introduction, I shared with him my concern about his schedule and ability to make our engagement a priority. He admitted he didn't realize so much time had passed and said, "I don't know what's happening with my schedule. I just go the next meeting on my calendar." That was how unconscious and fragmented his attention to this area had become. Among many, one of the costs of his unconsciousness about his schedule was that he had to wait three months to start a coaching engagement he really wanted.

A lot of hidden and unconscious patterns show up when we start to examine our schedules. When I ask clients to reflect on the "why" behind their commitments and then to feel into what it would be like to let some of them go, some deeply ingrained mental and emotional patterns can surface. When I asked my client Cathy to examine her schedule, she told me it was pretty easy for her to cut back on her work commitments but that she felt extremely anxious about letting anything go on her weekends, even though that was when she craved time the most. When I asked her to explore what it would feel like if she didn't attend one of the many sporting events her children had, or to say no to a family social function, she started to cry. She told me, "I can't imagine missing something, because I already feel guilty that I'm not home enough." It took courage for Cathy to drop into her emotional experience and give voice to the thought of feeling guilty that had clearly been weighing on her.

I asked, "Just so I'm clear, your weekends are so full because you give so much to work during the week?" Then she started crying more because hearing her words reflected back to her helped her gain even more clarity about how she had been unconsciously prioritizing work over everything else in her life, including her family and herself.

For people like Cathy, this awareness and making choices is where the rubber hits the road. She had been telling me how much she wanted to shift her experience of work and life and how much she could feel the power of presence when she had the space to tune into it. Through her own process of discovery, she realized something had to give if she was going to continue to deepen her presence. In this moment, in the face of her emotional and mental patterns rearing their heads, she was at a major choice point about how she was going to move forward.

Simply asking Cathy to examine her commitments and her assumptions about those commitments opened up a whole other layer of conditioning that she hadn't been aware of. She acknowledged that many of her commitments were rooted in her reactive tendency of complying. Saying no or prioritizing her time brought up deep concerns about not keeping people happy and potentially compromising relationships. Of course, we didn't resolve everything in one session, but bringing awareness to Cathy's conditioned pattern of saying yes too often gave her more information to inform her decision making. After our discussion, she bravely vowed to have a conversation with her manager and her family about some commitments she wanted to renegotiate. She was nervous but clear about what she needed and why.

In the tools part of this section, I will offer you ways to reflect on your calendar, but don't frame this issue of your schedule and time in terms of balance or time management, as I believe those to be triage for a deeper issue: our deeply ingrained conditioning or autopilot response. When we have the courage to examine our commitments and the motivation behind our commitments, then we often walk into a much bigger set of mental and emotional patterns that we can explore. I can almost guarantee that when you are really honest with yourself about why you do some of the things you do with your time, you will be surprised at how often you are operating in an unconscious, conditioned state.

Some of my most courageous moments of choice came from examining my schedule and commitments and deciding to align my time with my deepest priority: presence. I am not sitting in lotus pose all day, because my sons are involved in a wide variety of extracurricular activities. I also offer support to aging parents, give to our community, and am committed to keeping a strong marriage, all while running a business, so I know what it feels like to pulled in many directions. I turn down a lot of invitations to social events, potential clients, travel, and even family gatherings because I am very clear about what it takes to stay connected to sanity and presence. I got here by taking one decision at a time, continuing to overcommit and feeling the strain on my system, and then reevaluating. This is the dial you can turn over time, and the first thing you need is to stay connected to the courage of examining where you continue to operate on autopilot.

The Value of Prioritizing

When you look at where you put your time, money, and energy, it will reveal what is most important to you. I'm not suggesting there is a right or wrong place to spend your time, money, and energy, but the act of examining it will reveal a lot about what you value and how conscious you are of how you are expending precious resources. It is not unusual for us to say we value one thing, only to find out that our actions are in direct contradiction with or, at a minimum, not supporting our espoused values. The goal in examining our schedules and priorities is to be fully aware of what you're doing, then to use that awareness to potentially make different choices.

On my own journey, I have been motivated to put my money where my mouth is, so to speak, when it comes to awareness of how I spend my time, money, and energy. I couldn't continue to speak and teach about presence, clarity, and awareness if I wasn't willing to do the courageous work of looking honestly at how I was prioritizing my resources. So I started peeling back the layers.

After I examined my calendar and how I use my time, the next natural place for me to start exploring my unconscious conditioned patterns was in my relationship with money. I was drawn to this area of my life because it felt connected to everything. Money was a major driver for how I used my time, what decisions I made, how I worked, and the dynamics with my husband. So it seemed that if I could gain awareness in this area, it would be beneficial to all parts of my life. Money used to trigger me a lot, and I knew I needed support in exploring this area of my life, so I hired a money coach. She first helped me to gain clarity about what I needed, versus what I wanted, in my business. Having clarity about exactly how much money I needed, then having conscious awareness of what I wanted and why, gave me a sense of empowerment about how I prioritized my time and energy. Of course, our time, money, and energy are deeply intertwined, but in my process I examined all three separately and then looked at the whole picture of my overall vitality and how it impacted my abundance.

After I had been working with my money coach for about a year, it became obvious that my husband and I needed to examine our dynamic together, since the decisions I made in my business impacted our home life. Both of us were nervous to start, because money was a tense subject, but, in the spirit of clarity, we mustered up the courage and prioritized our time to explore our financial relationship. When we started working with our money coach together, we found out that each of us had a unique, unconscious, conditioned pattern when it came to how we thought about money, as well as a collective pattern we had created together after almost two decades of marriage. We met with our money coach monthly for about two years, had weekly "money dates" where we brought our collective awareness to our spending, and had hard conversations about our dynamic. It took both of us being willing to have the courage to examine our autopilot behavior and responses for us to ultimately be free from what was probably the hardest aspect of our marriage. We still come together almost weekly to review our spending, discuss our family's needs and wants, and plan for our future. By having the courage to look at our dynamic and prioritizing time for clarity, we have transformed the process of talking about money into one far more enjoyable and collaborative than it has ever been, which of course contributes to an overall positive dynamic in our house.

Again, this is your journey, and only you will know what and why you are prioritizing one thing over the other. As I tell my clients, it's not so much about making the "right" or "wrong" decision—just be very clear about what you're doing and be real with yourself about the why. I suspect when you are radically honest with yourself about your priorities, awareness itself will propel you into new action or decision making.

Tools for Claiming Space

Your ability to claim space for your sanity, clarity, and awareness is a vital part of coming off autopilot and into presence. The following tools may help you claim that space for yourself and your family.

Calendar Reflection

I adapted this exercise from Janice Marturano's book, *Finding the Space to Lead*. The process guides you to be in relationship with your upcoming schedule in ways you may not have experienced before. The exercise is to be done in a silent, still place, without the use of technology, so print out your upcoming weekly and monthly schedule. Then close your eyes, breathe, and center yourself before you engage in the reflection exercise.

When you are ready, look at each commitment on each day with as little preconceived judgment as you can, and notice what it feels like in your body as you imagine spending your time in each meeting or appointment. You may notice tension, frustration, or lightness. Your job is to notice the information or patterns that are revealing themselves as you acknowledge awareness. I don't want to get too prescriptive about it, but I suspect having conscious awareness of your calendar at this level will prompt further exploration of and shifts in your decision making. Many of my clients have transformed how they use their time, simply by turning their consciousness to how they are using their time.

The next step is to notice what is *not* on your calendar. What is missing that you need or wish was there? Time for yourself? Time with friends or family? Time to just be? Or time for the mundane or day-to-day requirements of life that tend to pile up? Each week, I schedule time on my calendar to engage with my upcoming schedule. I start by examining the upcoming week, then the two and three weeks after that, and that gives me enough time to adjust it if I need to. You can also use this tool with your family schedule. My husband and I gather with our kids to discuss our upcoming schedules, and together we identify what we want to adjust on, add to, or take off our calendar. This helps our kids feel empowered about how they use their time and sets them up to be conscious of their schedules when they are older. When we have space on our calendars, we have space to be present with our life and our activities.

Saying No

The power of saying no is brilliant, though it can conjure up all sorts of low-mind concerns, especially if you have a strong slant toward the reactive tendency of complying. If you aren't (yet) good at saying no, this will be a great place for you to experiment and really notice the conditioned thoughts and emotions when you stretch yourself in the name of claiming more space for yourself.

Saying no is a little easier when someone is inviting you to an activity or commitment that is not on your calendar. When you are really clear about what you need in terms of space and are clear about the reality of your calendar, then it is a heck of a lot easier to say no. When someone invites you to a social event or asks you to contribute your time, you can simply say, "I'm sorry, but I can't" or, "I'm unable to join you." There is no need to overexplain yourself, although notice the reactions in your body and low mind when you simply say no.

Once, when I was approached by my son's PTA group asking if I could be on the board, the words "no, I can't" flew out of my mouth with such clarity that it took even me by surprise. I followed up by saying, "I'm really clear about what time I have to volunteer, and I will offer it when I can, but I'm choosing to not participate on the board." Both women looked at me with what I perceived as shock, and, after a moment of what felt like awkward silence, one of them said, "Holy cow, I love how clear you are. Good for you!" I admit I walked away from the interaction noticing my low mind being concerned about the impression I had made, but, just as I do with the other content of my low mind, I noticed it and didn't take it too seriously. Instead, I walked away smiling about how clear I had been and how I had maintained an important boundary regarding my time.

White Space

White space time is a chunk of time you have reserved that does not have a predetermined agenda. This means that you block out time (ideally, one to four hours per week), but you don't make a decision about how you're going to use that time until you begin. The purpose of white-space time is quite simple. It is space for you to acknowledge presence first and ask yourself what you need. White space is the air pocket in your week so you don't drown by the time Friday rolls around.

When you begin your white-space time, close your eyes, take a few grounding breaths or meditate, and then ask yourself, "What do I need right now?" or, "What is it that I'm inspired to do?" Most of us rarely have time to think, so many of my clients use their white-space time to become present, and it gives them space to turn their attention to whatever situation needs it. Others use white-space time *not* to think, but simply to be, and at different times they use it to treat themselves to some indulgence, attend to important details they wouldn't typically have time for, or even take a nap. When you enter your white-space time and ask yourself, "What do I need right now?" your answer may surprise you. Many of my clients don't realize how tired they are until they start their white-space time. Others tune in and realize they are starving for some quiet, so they go and take a walk outside.

By consciously building white space into your schedule, you are putting a stake in the ground for presence and clarity. The hardest part of white space is getting it on your calendar and keeping it. You may be able to find only an hour the first time you try it, but if you are engaging with your calendar consciously, you will be able to incorporate more white space. Then you will notice how often you are scheduling over your white space and why. Again, all of these reflections will be great data for you to continue to examine your autopilot reactions and what different choices you may want to make.

Family White Space

Family white space is not too different from personal white space, but I wanted to share this tool with you because it has made a huge difference in the way my entire family makes choices about our time. The premise is that on the weekends, we try to create a day, or at least a portion of a day, for family white space. We block the time on our calendars and don't commit it to anyone and anything else and agree that it will be our family time, which includes a no-technology rule. Then we come together at the beginning of our time and everyone gets to answer "What do you need?" or "What would you like to do with our time?" Again, this gives our boys the opportunity to practice identifying and voicing their needs, as well as to practice the skills of compromise and prioritization.

Often, our answers vary: my husband wants to go on a bike ride, my sons have homework, and I want to see a movie. We engage in conversation about a way for all of us to get our needs met, as well as carving out some time for us to be together as a family. The conversation isn't always perfect, but we do it regularly enough that the boys have learned to manage their time on the weekend so they don't have to do homework and so there is room for us to go on a hike or a movie together. Sometimes we end up doing things separately, but we made the decision together. The idea behind family white space is that you carve out time to proactively decide together, so you aren't constantly going from one activity to another in a state of autopilot.

Aligning Action with Awareness

It is inevitable that when you deepen your inward awareness, you will start to see your external life differently. When we drop in and wake up, it is almost impossible not to reevaluate some aspects of life and work and feel inspired to align our life decisions to support awareness. As a result of being more present, most of my clients end up reevaluating some of their relationship patterns and how they have been operating at work.

One of the most common experiences people have when they consciously acknowledge presence and awareness is that they can't help but notice how *not* present other people are in their lives. My clients are often concerned about how difficult it will be to stay present when so many others around them are not. I tell them that waking up and staying present is a little bit like becoming clean and sober from an addiction. One of the first principles of staying sober is to create an environment where you have a chance at being successful. This means you may need to reevaluate some of your old relationships and honestly ask yourself how that relationship is supporting or detracting from your presence. It might also mean that you reevaluate how and where you spend your time. If you truly want to stay awake, then you will have to evoke the courage to align your actions, relationships, and decisions to support your newfound awareness.

Surrendering to Awareness

When we drop in and listen to our inner knowing, we can sometimes be surprised by what we learn or feel compelled to do. I had been working with my client Diane for about eighteen months, and during our time together she had shared how much she wanted to be a foster parent. She was a single woman, working a demanding job as a senior director at a multinational technology company, and barely had enough time to take care of herself, let alone a child. After Diane had made enough room in her schedule to complete the foster-parent approval process, she received a call from the state asking if she might be available to take in triplet infant boys whose mother had been addicted to drugs. The state was only evaluating all care options at this time, but the phone call caused her to dig deep and truly evaluate her priorities.

Diane wasn't sure she could take on three high-needs infants as a single, working woman, and the phone call from the state forced her to get very clear on what she wanted and her priorities. Diane did her due diligence and spoke to other foster parents, parents of multiples, and parents of addicted babies. After hearing about Diane's situation, nearly everyone told her, "Don't take the babies. It's going to be too much." I have to admit, when she talked to me about the situation, I had a twinge of panic about what she was getting herself into. On top of all that, Diane had recently been offered a promotion to general manager and knew she would really enjoy the role and that the new job would be great for her career. Yet she also knew that she could not take on a new job and take care of the triplets at the same time.

After spending time dropping in and getting clear on what was needed, she told the state she was willing to take the triplets. She told me, "Sara, I know this sounds crazy and goes against all rational logic, but I just know I need to do this." Diane had such clarity and conviction in her voice that I knew the awareness coming through her was beyond her logical or analytical mind. Don't get me wrong, she was still incredibly scared, but she moved forward despite her fear. She turned down the offer for the general manager position and immediately transformed her home, her schedule, and her whole life as she knew it in preparation for the boys. The whole time she was making these shifts, she didn't know how long she would be taking care of the babies. It could be for only a few weeks or months.

The commitment and courage that Diane displayed in aligning her action with the deeper awareness within her inspired many people. I was in awe watching the outpouring of support that came in for her and the babies. Coworkers delivered cribs, diapers, car seats, and food. Family and friends took shifts to help care for the infants. For months, Diane was overwhelmed by (and deeply appreciative of) all the support she received. Since I was also working with Diane's manager and some of her coworkers, I knew that on some level we were all prepared to prop her up against the natural exhaustion and overwhelm of suddenly being responsible for three high-needs infants.

But what actually happened surprised us all. Diane flourished in the face of her new responsibilities. She wasn't taken off center or overwhelmed. Instead, it was like she dropped into a new level of stability and groundedness. She showed up to work less reactive, more productive, and full of vitality. She looked physically more alive and beautiful than she already was. She told everyone how purposeful and clear she felt about her priorities and how much energy that gave her. She took the leap to align her life with awareness, and the outcome pleasantly surprised us all.

As I'm writing this, Diane is still caring for the boys, who are nearly three years old. Even though she didn't and still doesn't know the ultimate outcome for them, she continues to align her decisions, time, and relationships to support them. She continues to drop into new levels of clarity and awareness as the custody case unfolds, and holds the vision that she may be able to adopt the boys someday. Also, during the three years since she's had the boys, she's been promoted to general manager and has continued to have a very fulfilling career.

Diane's situation demonstrates the power not only of tuning into a deeper awareness, but also of surrendering and committing to it. We may not all have the opportunity or calling to care for foster children, but each of us has something that we know we are being called to. It may be as simple as the next courageous conversation with a loved one, or a shift in life priorities. It may be finally exploring the new career path that you've been longing for or taking up a creative endeavor that you often think about. It might even be as simple as creating a bit more space for you to turn your attention to awareness to see what is there. Courage is not just about the big, bold moves of life; rather, it exists equally in the moment-by-moment choices we make.

Courage is being radically honest with yourself about what you know. When you drop into presence and awareness, information reveals itself. The question then becomes: Do you want to acknowledge the information and align your external life to what you know? So many of my life decisions, particularly in this last decade, didn't make "sense" to my low mind. Luckily, though, I have been in relationship enough with my low mind to know the difference between its chatter and the guidance from my deeper essence and am so happy I have had the courage to shift my external life to align with awareness.

The path may not be comfortable or easy, but I suspect you will feel very good about taking any courageous step. Start exploring your capacity for courage with something that feels doable but not necessarily comfortable. What is one thing you can shift in your external world that would support your presence? What is one thing you know you need to look at or address? What do you need to make a little space for?

One of my clients answered this question by telling me he hadn't been to the doctor or dentist in years and was tired of worrying about what might be wrong with his health. He decided to take two days off work to go to various appointments and found out that, outside of a couple of fillings, he was healthy.

Another client started by creating space in her calendar to go and visit her father's gravesite. This was something she had been putting off, but when she dropped in, she knew she needed and wanted to spend time there. When she arrived, she immediately started to feel the sadness and emotion of his passing, but she had made the space to properly grieve, and, although she was tired, she told me she felt much better.

Never have I looked back on my life to regret a courageous decision or action I have taken. In fact, those are the times when I feel most alive and proud of how I walk my talk. Although presence and awareness are chock-full of the unknown, when you have the courage to explore, you will feel a vitality and aliveness that just might surprise you.

Tools for Aligning with Awareness

Aligning with awareness is first about becoming conscious of your environment and how it supports or doesn't support your presence. When you are aligning with awareness, the question becomes: What do you need in order to support your continued awareness?

Put Yourself in the Field of Presence

I deeply value efficiency, and on my own journey I found that one of the most efficient ways for me to deepen my presence was to put myself in the space of others who were clearer than I was at the time. For me, that meant when I tuned into my inner guidance, I felt inspired to prioritize attending certain retreats and workshops. When I dropped in, I was guided to be in the field of certain teachers and to read or listen, even if I didn't fully understand what they were saying. It took humility and commitment to continue to dedicate my time and awareness to concepts or teachings I didn't think made a lot of sense, but when I tuned into my experience of the teachings beyond my analytical mind, the teachings still resonated with part of me—I noticed I felt clearer and more grounded. I continually committed time, money, and energy to being a student.

What happened as I deepened my awareness was that I noticed I naturally wanted to be around people who supported presence. That meant that a few relationships I had with friends, clients, and colleagues came to an end, because ultimately what became most important to me was to be around people who supported clarity and awareness.

Take the Very Next Step

There may be times on your journey when you will feel scared about stepping into the unknown. Fear comes with the territory of full engagement, and the visceral experience of fear probably won't ever go away, but you will become used to it. I now think of visceral fear as a sign that I'm fully engaged in life. But if you are feeling overwhelmed by your experience or by the information you are receiving through tuning into awareness, anchor to your breath and remember that your only job is to handle the very next step in front of you.

One of my clients became increasingly aware that her marriage was not healthy. When she thought about divorce, she became paralyzed with fear. Instead of staying paralyzed, she decided to take one step at a time. She found a place to stay when she was ready, met with a divorce attorney, set up a new checking account, and continued to make space to be with her fear and sadness. All of her actions took months, but eventually she found herself ready to file for divorce.

When we look too far out in front of the present moment, the unknown can cloud our clarity, so remember that you need only to take the next step, and you will know what to do when the next step after that reveals itself.

Get Support

Since I'm a coach, it is no wonder that I fully encourage anyone to get the support they need to make a change in their life. People hire personal trainers for their physical health all the time, so why not seek out support for your emotional, mental, and spiritual health and growth? When we operate on autopilot, we simply don't know what we don't know, and it is important to find ways to help us become aware of our blind spots.

It doesn't mean you have to spend thousands of dollars to get support. If you are sincere about your intention for clarity and prioritize your time, energy, and money, I suspect the support will reveal itself to you. As the old saying goes, "When the student is ready, the teacher will appear." The support may come in the form of a teacher, an experience, a group of people, or just an "out of the blue" knowing. What I know for sure, though, is that whenever a teacher (person or experience) revealed itself to me, I had to dig deep and decide just how serious I was about my commitment to learning and presence. I was invited to make some very powerful and bold choices to work with some teachers, and every one of those choices scared the heck out of me. In retrospect, though, I realize that every decision I made gave me a bigger return on my investment than I could ever have imagined. Every teacher helped me in turning my awareness to presence and then ultimately experiencing the stability that comes from presence. I honestly don't think I could have made it to where I am now without the customized support of the dozens of coaches, teachers, and guides who helped me along the way.

Body Integration

When we drop into the experience of our head, heart, and gut and become more conscious of our conditioned patterns, it's likely that our thoughts, feelings, and behaviors will shift to being more productive and healthy. However, it's imperative that we drop in deep enough to explore how the pattern is ingrained in our physical body. The ways we walk, talk, think, and act are rooted in our body, so we often need to bring our attention to our body to fully unlock a pattern.

Body integration work can take on a variety of forms. Some modalities for integrating the body into consciousness work are craniosacral, acupuncture, somatic body work, Rolfing, reiki, yoga, and massage. Although this is not an exhaustive list of modalities to integrate healing in the physical body, these approaches are available in most major cities.

The reason I love body integration work is that it gives me yet another doorway to awareness. Through body work, I have become aware of how my body reflects my emotional and mental patterns, and when I notice myself tensing up in my hips or feel tightness in my shoulders, I have yet another way of exploring my experience in the moment. My body has become a vital and important source of data for me and has allowed me to quickly gain clarity about my patterns. In the cases of energy healing work and craniosacral therapy, I notice that even if I don't intellectually know what is shifting in the session, I often come away from it with a heightened sense of awareness and clarity I didn't have before.

Part Two Reflection

This section guided you through the experience of dropping into your clear mind, connected heart, and courageous gut. Dropping in fundamentally rests on the foundation of presence and awareness, and then, from that foundation, you will be guided to the resources and experiences that will support you in moving from conditioned pattern to presence. Here are some of the key points from this section:

- Stability and groundedness reside in acknowledging the constant still and quiet nature of presence.
- In order to work with any of our patterns, we must first access stable ground so we won't get swept away by emotion or thought.
- In order to access a clear mind, we need to gather our attention through some sort of inward reflection or what I referred to in this section as meditation.
- Question mind stories by externalizing the story, asking, "What if this wasn't about me?" and by checking the accuracy of the story.
- When we connect to our heart, the experience of love is a natural and organic expression of presence.
- Listening is one of the best ways to connect to ourselves and others.
- Deep listening requires a spirit of nondoing, nonknowing, and nonattachment.
- We can connect to our heart through gratitude, assuming decent intent and goodwill meditation.
- Courage is moving forward, even in the face of fear. When in overwhelm, look to the very next opportunity and just take things one step at a time.
- We need space and quiet to drop in and explore our inner experience.
- The ways we spend our time, money, and energy will reveal our current priorities.
- We have the opportunity to experience courage when we explore aligning our action with awareness.

As you made your way through this book, especially through this last part, notice how (or whether) your experience has shifted. Do you feel more inspired, nervous, or clear? The act of prioritizing and sticking with the digesting of this book is an act of courage and clarity. The more you engage in your own inward journey, the more you will be led to the next opportunity for liberation.

Ideas or Reflections

_____
_____
_____
_____
_____
_____
_____
_____
_____
_____
_____
_____
_____
_____
_____
_____
_____
_____
_____
_____
_____
_____

CHAPTER 7—Going Forward in the World

There's no need to travel anywhere. Journey within yourself. —Rumi

IF, YEARS AGO, SOMEONE HAD given me the choice of embarking on a long journey of twists and turns, full of losses and gains, with an uncertain outcome but with the promise of feeling the way I do today, versus sticking with the status quo, it's likely that I would have chosen the latter. Back then, I had no idea what opportunities for deepened awareness and presence lay ahead of me, especially that morning when I woke up with the right side of my face paralyzed from Bell's palsy. When I look back on it now, as with any journey, I realize the richness of the experience was in the not knowing, and then in making choice after choice toward what a deep part of me longed for: presence. Of course, no one actually offered me the "choice" of going on the journey to presence; instead, the journey revealed itself to me.

Tell Me What to Do

It's normal when thinking about your own journey to want to grasp onto something to "do." I had been working with my client Alex for a few months when I noticed that he came to nearly every session with some version of the same request: "Tell me what to do." I appreciated Alex's desire to understand and engage, but I also knew I couldn't direct him. I suspected that Alex was operating from his old, reactive patterns of control.

This reactive pattern came to a head when he told me in one session that he was so frustrated that he was at a breaking point. He was frustrated that he couldn't get on top of his calendar and commitments, that he had no time with his wife, that he wasn't doing "better" in our coaching. When he looked outside himself, he felt anything but successful. His tension was palpable, and he seemed on the verge of a breakthrough, although for Alex it might have felt more like being on the verge of a breakdown. I reflected back to him what I was seeing, saying, "It looks like no matter how hard you try, you aren't able to control all aspects of your life." I realized this statement would be slightly provoking (as I knew about his deep pattern of control), but I also hoped it might allow all his pent-up emotion to start to move.

With complete exasperation, he looked at me and said, "I'm screwed."

I knew Alex wasn't "screwed," but his low mind was working to convince him that his "failure" to hold it all together was devastating. What really happened was that Alex's conditioning was finally unraveling, which to his low mind felt feel like failure, or even like a death of sorts.

After a good fight, Alex's low mind finally surrendered. Once he said, "I'm screwed," the energy shifted and our conversation ended up being one of the most rich, open, and honest ones we'd had to date. Alex felt relieved that he was no longer trying to keep it all together and told me how much better he felt after our session.

After a week, he e-mailed me to tell me how different his week had been. He finally asked for support at work, took a few things off his calendar, and booked a couple of date nights with his wife. Suddenly, he knew exactly what to do without my telling him.

It's not necessarily a bad thing that your mind wants to know what to do. However, I would encourage you to honestly explore your desire to have something to do and to investigate whether that desire is really your low mind's attempt to understand, control, or manipulate your experience. I suspect if you truly drop into your clear mind, connected heart, and courageous gut, you, too, will know exactly what to do next.

The Hero's Journey

The process of waking up from our conditioned, autopilot state requires full commitment. Commitment means that you continue coming back to presence and mustering up the courage to explore and align your actions with it. When you are committed, you take the next step in front of you, knowing the journey is long and not needing to know exactly where it's going. Mythology researcher Joseph Campbell documented common patterns or story arcs that run through thousands of historic myths and stories from around the world. In his book *The Hero with a Thousand Faces*, he outlines common stages that every "hero" goes through, regardless of the type of story or culture the hero originates from. Campbell calls this common structure a monomyth, also known as the hero's journey. Although the hero's journey is rooted in myth, it also correlates closely with the journey of awakening, or increasing consciousness, and the commitment required to take the journey.

If you look at movies like *Star Wars*, *The Wizard of Oz*, and *Harry Potter*, or classic tales such as *The Hobbit* or *Alice's Adventures in Wonderland*, you will see the common story arc of the hero's journey. Campbell outlines three basic phases that make up the hero's journey: the Separation, the Initiation, and the Return.[10] The Separation phase begins when the hero or heroine is called into an "adventure," where they become aware of a different and often strange world beyond what they have known. Sometimes this happens by accident, and sometimes the hero is summoned to seek something external, such as a treasure or a loved one. In nearly every story or myth, the hero initially refuses the call to adventure because they don't believe they are equipped for the journey, or because they are reluctant to leave their family and friends in their current world. Resistance to, or even refusal to engage in, the quest is a common and important part of the Initiation stage. Campbell outlines that during the Initiation phase, the hero is given a quest that only they can do because of their unique skills, powers, or destiny. The hero often accepts the quest when they are emotionally motivated to do so.

For example, although Dorothy in *The Wizard of Oz* finds herself in a strange land, she ultimately accepts her quest in order to get back "home." Luke Skywalker's quest in *Star Wars* starts when he realizes his aunt and uncle have been killed. In all of the classic tales, the heroes find themselves no longer having an option to stay in the status quo.

Once they accept their quest or journey, the hero steps consciously into the unknown but lacks any awareness of what they will have to face. Although scared, the hero bravely enters the journey with nothing more than their current skill, power, and commitment to move forward. Campbell shares that during the Initiation phase, the hero will receive aid from a variety of sources, such as a mentor or guide, like Yoda, or from allies or helpers, like the Scarecrow, the Tin Man, and the Cowardly Lion. The hero will be given the support, training, or tools they need to be prepared for their ultimate challenge or test.

Along the journey, the hero must always complete the quest on their own, because ultimately they will have to integrate all that they have learned. Campbell refers to this requirement as the "supreme ordeal." For example, Harry Potter was the only one who could fight and ultimately destroy the villain Voldermort because Harry was the "chosen one." Although he had plenty of help, support, and mentoring along the way, only he could face the "supreme ordeal" in each story.

When the hero successfully conquers the supreme ordeal, they have entered the third stage, the Return. During this stage, the hero returns home and is often rewarded or celebrated for their courage and endurance. Also during this stage, it is revealed how life-changing the journey was for the hero and for those around them. They often experience a feeling that their old world hasn't changed but the hero has. At the end of *Alice's Adventures in Wonderland*, Alice wakes up from a "dream" and questions whether what she experienced was real. Although she is unsure, both Alice and the reader sense that the experience has changed her in a profound way. Heroes often return from their journeys with a newfound maturity or clarity as they realize that their journey has forever altered them and they begin to own their powers or gifts.[11]

Although the hero's journey is rooted in myth and story, the same story arc reveals itself in "real" life. If we were to examine the life journeys of impactful political and social-change leaders, such as Dr. Martin Luther King, Jr., or Pakistani education activist Malala Yousafzai, we would see that both of them were called to a journey that at first they didn't necessarily choose. Instead, they both found themselves in the middle of injustice and at a crossroads between being a victim of the injustice and following their inner calling to lead. Although I don't know each of their stories intimately, I suspect that at the beginning of these heroes' journeys, they didn't know where the path would lead or even imagine that they would become the heroes they are today. They didn't choose the journey for the outcome—the journey chose them—and they became heroes because they had the courage to follow their inner knowing.

Like our own journey toward presence and awareness, the hero's journey unfolds as the hero finds out that the stakes get a little higher with every step. The hero is continually confronted with the option of going with the safe, predictable route or opting to muster up courage and venture into the unknown. The experience of choosing the journey evokes higher levels of awareness, courage, strength, and ultimately results in the hero's realizing their potential. Similar to our own path toward presence, the hero's journey reveals that what the hero thought they were seeking—something outside themselves—was only the initial motivation to launch them on the journey, not the ultimate prize of understanding their deeper potential.

The reason why I and many who study the hero's journey find it so universally understood is that it touches on our own knowing that we each have an epic journey in front of us if we so choose. We all have the opportunity to step bravely into the unknown and to explore our deeper potential on this planet. If you think about all of the heroes documented throughout history and across genres, like each of us, they have unique vulnerabilities and struggles, and even make what appear to be mistakes or "bad" decisions. Their vulnerability, courage, and commitment demonstrate to us what is possible when we move bravely toward our own journey of awakening. The truth and possibility we encounter when we read about the hero's journey or see it play out resonate with us.

You may not consider yourself a hero or heroine, but if you engage in any level of self-reflection and deepening your relationship with awareness, you have initiated your own hero's journey. If you notice along this path that is uniquely yours that you aren't sure you have what it takes, or where to go next, or even if you want to be on this journey at all, know that your reluctance is one stage of the journey, too, and trust yourself to keep going and to follow the call to something deeper, to see where it leads. I suspect that you, too, will be given the support, guidance, and tools you need to navigate the unknown road ahead, just as every hero before you has.

Own Your Journey

Remember that your life is *your* journey and that you must rely on your inner guidance to know what is right for you. Try to avoid comparing where you are with where other people are, or what path you take with that of anyone else around you, as it will likely set you up for frustration and further judgment. Instead, own your journey with much fervor.

I don't know how many times I have felt unsure or questioned the heck out of myself because I was choosing something different than those around me did. But when it came down to it, my inner knowing was and still is the most reliable tool I have to navigate my life and external choices. No matter what external circumstances I have faced, I've always been able to rely on the stability of my inner knowing to guide me. That stability alone has been worth any of the difficult parts of the journey.

Referring back to the tenets at the beginning of the book may help you with a little stability and support as you make your bold and courageous moves toward the journey of presence. And, if nothing else, know there is at least one person who is metaphorically standing next to you, cheering you on, as you embark on your own journey. (That's me!)

As you engage in dropping into deeper presence and courage, don't underestimate the impact you will have on the world. Your family, friends, coworkers, and community members will feel your clarity, strength, and love, often without your "doing" anything. You will be continually surprised by just how much you have inspired others with your courage and willingness to embark on your epic journey toward presence and ultimate liberation. In closing, I offer these words and energy to you:

May you be happy.
May you be at peace.
May you be free.

Notes

I WROTE ALL CLIENT STORIES in this book based on actual client experiences, although in some cases I used a composite story based on several similar client experiences, and in other cases I referenced very specific client stories. In every case, I have changed the client's name to protect their identity.

Much of this book is based on my personal journey and on learning from the various sources, coaches, and teachers I have encountered along the way. I not have cited every source to enhance readability, but I've cited all major contributors to the content of the book. In recent years, my own development and the way I work with clients has been highly influenced by the teachings of both Adyashanti, at Open Gate Sanga, and the Leadership Circle. It would be difficult to list all the ways in which they have influenced my work, but I reference their bodies of work regularly throughout the book.

Chapter 1

1. David M. Sanbonmatsu, David L. Strayer, Nathan Medeiros-Ward, and Jason M. Watson, "Who Multi-Tasks and Why? Multi-Tasking Ability, Perceived Multi-Tasking Ability, Impulsivity, and Sensation Seeking," 2013, http://journals.plos.org/plosone/article?id=10.1371/journal.pone.0054402#s4.

2. Timothy Wilson et al., series of eleven studies, 2014, https://news.virginia.edu/content/doing-something-better-doing-nothing-most-people-study-shows.

3. Boundless.com, "The Limbic System," https://www.boundless.com/psychology/textbooks/boundless-psychology-textbook/biological-foundations-of-psychology-3/structure-and-function-of-the-brain-35/the-limbic-system-154-12689/.

4. Judson A. Brewer et al., "Meditation experience is associated with differences in default mode network activity and connectivity," 2011, http://www.pnas.org/content/108/50/20254.long.

5. Caroline C. Ross, "Do Anti-depressants Really Work?" 2012, http://www.psychologytoday.com/blog/real-healing/201202/do-anti-depressants-really-work.

Chapter 2

6. Joe Dispenza, *You Are the Placebo* (New York: Hay House Publishing, 2015).

Chapter 3

7. Wikipedia, Karen Horney entry, https://en.wikipedia.org/wiki/Karen_Horney.

8. Robert J. Anderson and William A. Adams, *Mastering Leadership* (New York: Wiley, 2015).

Chapter 4

9. Sanbonmatsu et al.

Chapter 7

10. Lynne Milum, "The Hero's Journey," 2003, http://www.mythichero.com/what_is_mythology.html.

11. Mythology Teacher.com, "The Hero's Journey," http://mythology teacher.com/documents/TheHeroJourney.pdf.

Acknowledgments

WHEN I SET OUT TO WRITE this book nearly three years ago, I had no idea that the process of writing about presence would propel me into my own hero's journey toward presence. Luckily, several people were there not only to support the writing of this book, but also, more important, to support me as I walked my own path of presence so I could write about it from a place of experience.

Brooke Warner, my editor, and publisher of She Writes Press, has guided me for years with a keen eye, an open heart, and sheer brilliance as I have muddled through my creative process. She has challenged me to go deeper, supported me when I needed to take breaks, and stewarded my thought process through what has been my most epic creative endeavor so far. I'm confident this book would not be what it is without her guidance and support, and I'm forever grateful.

I'm also deeply appreciative for the guidance and support I've received from my friend, colleague, and guide Pamela Saari. Her solid presence and clarity led me to levels of awareness I didn't know existed and gave me the courage to repeatedly surrender to presence. I'm also very grateful for the hours she spent with me reviewing each chapter, challenging my messaging, cheering me on when I needed it, and supporting the entire project to unfold in its time. It's a true gift to have someone in your life who can see what you cannot and who can guide you to your own clarity without any judgment or agenda.

A big thank-you to my prereaders, Jesse, Jeanie, Lisa, Gustavo, Heather, and Lisa. Your feedback helped fine-tune my writing and concepts. Having your consistent feedback and support made all the difference as I ran toward the finish line with this project. Also, thank you to Crystal Patriarche and the entire She Writes Press and BookSparks team. You all have supported me, my message, and my platform throughout its continued emergence and shifts in these last couple of years. I appreciate your patience and tenacity in sticking with me on this journey.

Thank you to my dear husband, Jesse, and our wonderful sons, Ethan and Logan. You have been incredibly patient with my process of growing and learning, as well as writing. You support me with your love, humor, and presence, and you create a sanctuary where I feel safe and fulfilled. Each of you has inspired me with your wisdom and your love has helped me to continually step into the unknown.

To my family and friends, who are such a loving presence in my life: you make this journey more fun, engaging, and meaningful. Mom and Dad, I would not be here without you and I'm grateful for the solid foundation and the freedom to launch into my future with gusto.

Last, to my clients, it is a true honor to walk next to you and witness your unfolding in such consistent and profound ways. Your vulnerability and strength never cease to amaze me, and you are the true inspiration for this book.